Flawless

Flawless

Understanding Faults in Wine

JAMIE GOODE

UNIVERSITY OF CALIFORNIA PRESS

University of California Press, one of the most distin-
guished university presses in the United States, enriches
lives around the world by advancing scholarship in the
humanities, social sciences, and natural sciences. Its
activities are supported by the UC Press Foundation and
by philanthropic contributions from individuals and
institutions. For more information, visit www.ucpress.edu.

University of California Press
Oakland, California

Library of Congress Cataloging-in-Publication Data

Names: Goode, Jamie, author.
Title: Flawless : understanding faults in wine /
    Jamie Goode.
Description: Oakland, California : University of
    California Press, [2018] | Includes bibliographical
    references and index. |
Identifiers: LCCN 2018000772 (print) | LCCN 2018004514
    (ebook) | ISBN 9780520971318 (Ebook) |
    ISBN 9780520276901 (cloth)
Subjects: LCSH: Wine and wine making.
Classification: LCC TP548 (ebook) | LCC TP548 .G62595 2018
    (print) | DDC 663/.2—dc23

LC record available at https://lccn.loc.gov/2018000772

27 26 25 24 23 22 21 20 19
10 9 8 7 6 5 4 3

Table of Contents

Acknowledgments

Many people have contributed ideas to this book. First, I'd like to thank Sam Harrop MW, a long-time collaborator. When I was just starting out in wine writing in the early noughties, Sam gave me a lead on the growing trend of toying with reductive characters to increase wine complexity. This was all very new, and I began researching and writing about it. Some years later, we decided we'd like to write a book together on wine faults. Sam, however, is in great demand as a consultant winemaker, and the project faltered, but not until the title of the book was chosen (it was Sam's idea) and the concept of *wabi sabi*—taking a more nuanced, thoughtful look at wine "faults"—was established as a philosophical underpinning to this complex topic. Without Sam this book wouldn't exist, and I'm grateful for his significant input to the development of some of the ideas here.

Second, I'd like to thank the staff at the Australian Wine Research Insititute (AWRI)—in particular Peter Godden, who reviewed the manuscript for UC Press—for the assistance they have given me. I've visited the AWRI a few times over the years, and I've always been impressed by the quality of their research and by how practical and topical it is. A lot of wine research is worthy but not always that relevant to the production of interesting wine, but theirs is goal focused and has made a very positive contribution to helping winemakers across Australia make better wines. I'm grateful to all the AWRI staff who've given their time to speak to me.

I'd also like to thank the team at Lallemand, a forward-thinking yeast and bacteria company. For the last few years, I have been part of their consultant group that meets to discuss new product development and various aspects of microbial wine science. Through this group I have learned a lot. (Conflict-of-interest disclosure: I am paid for my time participating in these meetings and for presenting lectures at Lallemand-sponsored events.)

As a wine journalist and communicator, I spend a lot of time on the road visiting wine regions. It's through the openness and generosity of winegrowers around the world, who are prepared to give up substantial chunks of time to let me see what they are up to, that I have been able to learn so much and to develop the context that puts the insights of wine science into appropriate perspective. This sort of context is extremely valuable. It needs to be remembered that there's only so much funding for science and that, because of the complexity of wine, the experiences and anecdotal observations of keen winegrowers are extremely useful. I would like to thank all those who have generously allowed me to invade their cellars and vineyards and who have been open to sharing their insights.

Thanks also to Chris Ashton and the team at the International Wine Challenge, where I have been a panel chair and more recently a cochair for several years now. The experience of tasting so many wines, and latterly of reviewing all the wines declared faulty by the tasting tables, has been invaluable.

I am also grateful to those who have given extended interviews, including but not limited to Andrew Waterhouse (who read and commented on the chapter on oxidation), Roger Boulton, Adrian Coulter, Dominique Delteil, and Maurizio Ugliano. I thank the scientists in New Zealand who allowed me to interview them while I was working on a project on the science of Sauvignon Blanc—many of their insights were relevant to this book.

Thanks to Belinda Kemp of Cool Climate Oenology and Viticulture Institute (CCOVI), Brock University, Canada for reading and commenting on the manuscript at peer review stage. Her suggestions were very useful and improved the text.

As a freelance wine communicator, I depend on the people who believe in me enough to commission work, to hire me to talk or judge wine, and to sponsor wineanorak.com, my website. Naturally, I'm thankful to all those who pay me cash! It is much appreciated.

Finally, thank you to all at UC Press for doing such a good job. No book is perfect, but the peer-review and editing process made this a much better book than it would otherwise have been. Every author needs a good editor.

CHAPTER ONE

Introduction

Wine is complicated. Almost impossibly so.

It's the result of microbial fermentation, guided by human hands, based on a natural starting product that's harvested once a year. The grapes differ markedly from season to season, and the nature of the vineyard site—the soil and climate the grape vine grows in—differs markedly over a short distance. Differences in geography and grape variety, compounded by human choices, result in a bewildering array of commercial wines. There's no product quite like it.

Because of the variability in the starting material—the grapes and microbes—winemakers can't easily follow a formula. They need to make the appropriate choices and interventions during the winemaking process in order to produce a marketable wine they are proud to stand behind. Commercial and market considerations often enter the fray. It's not a simple process.

Because nature and chance play such a significant role in wine production, it's not surprising that wine quality varies. And sometimes wines are faulty. The incidence of wines declared by professionals to be faulty in major competitions such as the International Wine Challenge is unacceptably high and probably wouldn't be tolerated in any other industry. And these are wines that have made it all the way to bottle. It's impossible to be sure how many "faulty" wines are consumed each year; it's likely that most of these are drunk, but not enjoyed, without the consumer realizing that the wine isn't supposed to taste this way.

Hence this book. It may seem a little negative to write a book on wine faults. After all, who likes to focus on flaws or errors? Does it mean the book will be a bit of a downer? Will its sales stagnate, even if it should prove to be an important text, simply because people are turned off by the term *fault?*

I hope not, and I deliberately chose the title—*Flawless*—to emphasize the positive. The absence of flaws may not actually be a positive quality in itself, but flaws prevent positive attributes of a wine from being enjoyed. It is by avoiding flaws that winemakers are free to achieve their goal. Beauty is marred by flaws, so their avoidance is a worthy aspiration. But the reality is a little more layered and complex than this. Sometimes, small levels of what might at higher levels be fault compounds can help beauty express itself—a theme I will return to several times in this book.

Beauty itself is much more than simply the avoidance of faults. To use a slightly religious-sounding analogy, there is more to virtue than an absence of sin. A wine may be flawless yet desperately dull. So my remit in writing this book is to go beyond simply the avoidance of faults and to touch on the semiphilosophical question of the nature of beauty as it applies to wine. As well as the traditional roster of faults, I will include more novel (and perhaps controversial) categories.

WINE FAULTS ARE INTERESTING

The topic of wine faults is of great interest. It's a rich, nuanced, complicated subject that strays from wine chemistry through microbiology to human perception and quality judgments. Some faults are universally agreed on: I can't see many people arguing a strong case for cork taint by 2,4,6-trichloroanisole (widely known simply as TCA) being a "complexing factor." Other faults are more a question of degree and personal preference: the spicy, medicinal, animal savoriness imparted by *Brettanomyces* yeast is a great example.

Some make a distinction between faults and taints. Defined as resulting from the fermentation process, faults include oxidation, *Brettanomyces,* volatile acidity, and reduction. A taint, in this classification scheme, is when a wine is affected by an extraneous flavor chemical, such as cork taint, eucalyptus taint, or smoke taint. "Faults are generally internal," says Adrian Coulter of the Australian Wine Research Institute, "like something microbial, or something wrong with the wine. Taints are something coming from the outside. It might still be something in the winemaking: for example, a wine additive might be tainted with a compound, and you add it to the wine, and it taints it." In this book, I refer to both categories as "faults."

Looking for the Positives

I hope that the overall tone of this book will be rather positive. I also hope that reading it will inspire winemakers to be more creative, and not just more defensive, in their winemaking. It is through a full understanding of faults, their origins, and their complexity—acknowledging that the presence of a specific character can be negative in some wines but positive in others—that wine-makers can leave the overly defensive path that can result in rather sterile, clean but uninspiring, technically correct wines.

Some wines are clearly faulty to all. Others split opinion. This will be a recurring theme as I examine faults one by one. Who gets to decide whether a wine is faulty or not? That's a good question, and we may have to leave the rather handy dualistic division between faulty and correct wines and move to a worldview that offers more of a continuum—at least for those wines that fall into the gray area between the two firm positions. And it looks like we will not be able to make the following pronouncement: If a wine contains chemical x at a level greater than $y \mu g/L$, then it is faulty. It turns out there are only a limited number of instances where this sort of rule makes sense.

The Science behind Faults

While a lot of good research on wine faults has been published in peer-reviewed scientific journals, there is much that is still not documented in rigorous scientific terms. So I haven't restricted my research to the published literature. This book will include the experiences of winemakers from around the globe. These people, day in and day out, come face to face with wine faults, and their accumulated experience is a valuable source of information. On many of the topics, an honest answer will be "We suspect ... " or even "We just don't know."

PERFECTION VERSUS IMPERFECTION: ON THE NATURE OF BEAUTY

I want to introduce a concept that I think is really helpful for understanding wine faults, and for grasping the notion that some flavor chemicals can be both faulty and positive, depending on the concentration and the context. This is the Japanese concept of *wabi-sabi*. Put in simple terms, it is the idea that flaws can bring out beauty, or that flaws are in fact part of beauty. In contrast to the Western aesthetic of striving for a beauty that lies in the attainment (or near attainment) of perfection, wabi-sabi suggests that beauty is transient, incomplete, and imperfect. Features that are not beautiful in and of themselves can contribute to beauty, and the wabi-sabi aesthetic—in many ways a more satisfying and richer one—includes characteristics such as asymmetry, irregularity, simplicity, economy, modesty, and austerity. The idea of applying wabi-sabi to wine faults came from my discussions with Sam Harrop, who should get the credit.

Wine consultant Ken Ohashi introduced Sam and me to a Japanese term that translates as "silence like a drop of water." Imagine you are sitting by a pool in a zen garden. It is as silent and tranquil as you can get. But it's the sound of water drops that shows you how silent it is—without this subtle noise, you wouldn't have recognized and appreciated the silence. Another example is the gentle ticking of a mechanical clock in an otherwise silent room: it seems to emphasize the quietness. Ohashi gives the example of a red wine that he tried, with some matchstick and pepper reductive characters. He describes these as the "minerality" of the wine, without which he thinks it would have tasted simple and even watery. But the presence of these traces of what could be called a wine fault—reduction—allowed him to see the purity of the wine. In the absence of the reduction, he wouldn't have recognized the purity.

Perfumers are familiar with the idea that smells that are highly aversive on their own can be useful in creating a beautiful perfume. One of the most expensive ingredients in perfume is ambergris, which is taken from what is the whale equivalent of a cat's fur ball (it is produced in the digestive system of sperm whales). This is actually quite disgusting, and smelled alone it would be repellent. But in a mix of odors, it provides interest and complements other, more immediately attractive smells while acting as a fixer, helping the aromas of the perfume persist. Another example is the aroma of jasmine. It contains small amounts of indole, which on its own would be an aversive smell. If people smell synthetic jasmine (which doesn't have indole) and the real thing (which does), often they can't tell them apart. But if they are pressed to decide which they prefer, they frequently opt for the real thing: the trace of the normally aversive indole adds something that people like to the smell of jasmine.

In a similar vein, let's consider music. What makes it beautiful? Music follows mathematical order, but not perfectly—that would be very boring. In a study published in a leading scientific journal, *Nature Neuroscience*,[1] the authors showed that music causes the release of the reward chemical dopamine in the brain, as do other pleasurable stimuli like food, drugs, and sex. They also showed that this dopamine release occurs both at peak emotional moments in the music—the "good bits," such as a melodic hook or chorus—and in anticipation of those good bits. The authors state:

> The anticipatory phase, set off by temporal cues signaling that a potentially pleasurable auditory sequence is coming, can trigger expectations of euphoric emotional states and create a sense of wanting and reward prediction. This reward is entirely abstract and may involve such factors as suspended expectations and a sense of resolution. Indeed, composers and performers frequently take advantage of such phenomena, and manipulate emotional arousal by violating expectations in certain ways or by delaying the

predicted outcome (for example, by inserting unexpected notes or slowing tempo) before the resolution to heighten the motivation for completion.

Good composers and songwriters leave us unfulfilled. They tease us, showing us briefly the notes or chord that we want to hear and then avoiding it until the main hook or chorus. They build up expectation, and may even seek to diffuse the expectation by putting in unexpected notes or chords. In a sense, they create something more beautiful by avoiding the obvious expression of what we would classify as beauty. And the "flaws" or "deviations" highlight the beauty when it is finally revealed. Or perhaps they go deeper: the flaws and deviations may well be part of the beauty.

We find the same dynamic in the arena of flavor. Tasted alone, salt is not pleasant. It's aversive. But at the appropriate level it adds life to food, creating a tension. The same goes for lemon juice: alone it is too acidic to be pleasurable for most people, but it creates a needed tension in some dishes. Sweetness alone is cloying; counter it with adequate acidity and it's lovely.

Our attraction to faces is a further example of the complex nature of beauty. There are certain rules of facial attractiveness in humans, and the evidence suggests they are hardwired. For example, judgments of facial beauty are cross-culturally consistent among adults and children, and young babies will look longer at attractive faces than at less attractive ones. It's not an absolute property; it's just that there are guidelines governing what sort of faces people find desirable, and evolutionary explanations for why this might be so. Certainly, a beautiful face is something we find very compelling. Yet attempts by scientists to produce the "perfect" one result in a composite face that, while certainly striking and attractive, looks slightly bland and *less* attractive than you'd expect. It's the presence of subtle flaws that brings out the real beauty. We love faces with a bit of character, not a total absence of even the smallest flaws. Most of all, though, we are attracted to the faces of those we know and like.

How does this relate to wine? I will argue that the most attractive, compelling wines are those that have elements of their character that, if they were in a different context or present at higher levels, might be considered faulty. It all depends on the wine, the context, and the consumer. When is volatile acidity too high? When is greenness good and when is it too bad? When are tannins too grippy and firm? When are earthy, spicy characters off-putting? When is savoriness or gaminess too prominent? When is new oak too obtrusive? When does a wine pass from mature to senescent? Many of these characters are present to a degree in some of the world's greatest wines. These are the sorts of questions I will address in subsequent chapters.

DEFINING "FAULT"

What exactly constitutes a fault in a wine is a matter of some contention. In part, it's subjective: some people enjoy a wine that has high levels of *Brettanomyces* or volatile acidity, while others find these objectionable if they are detectable. So a first-pass definition would be a subjective one: a wine fault is defined as the presence of a chemical compound (or combination of compounds) that detracts from wine quality. And here I would define *quality* as fitness for purpose. Thus, a faulty wine is one that a consumer dislikes (or likes less than they otherwise would) because of the presence of the negative quality. Faultiness could include, for example, excessive green characters and acidity owing to unripeness, or excessive sweet vanilla and coconut characters stemming from too much oak use. It is clear that this is a subjective definition, because some people like oak flavors more than others, and some prefer sweet ripe fruit more than others and are less tolerant of greenness in their wines. Thus, a wine can be faulty to one person and not to another. And faultiness is a continuum: wine quality is gradually lost, for example, as the wine shows more *Brettanomyces* character, even for those who quite like (sometimes without realizing what it is) *Brettanomyces* in their wine. This makes the whole issue of faults quite complicated.

A second, somewhat more objective definition is based on an "average" taster—one with average sensitivity to all potential fault compounds, along with the educated ability to recognize them when they are encountered in wine. This definition will require some sort of global consensus on the acceptable limits of the various fault compounds in wine. For example, a musty taint, such as cork taint, would be unacceptable at any detectable level. *Brettanomyces* might be considered acceptable at certain levels in some wine contexts—such as in ripe Mediterranean red wines, to which it adds spice and savoriness without dominating—but not in others, such as Pinot Noir, where it rarely works. This is a complicated and somewhat controversial approach, but it's not impossible. It's how we tend to operate in the wine trade and in wine competitions. We recognize that individual tasters differ in their biology and preferences, yet we aim at a universal standard of wine quality, which we then reward. It's not perfect, but it seems to work fairly well most of the time.

Attempting to define faults precisely is difficult and perilous, for sure. But to rely on subjective definitions creates the absurdity of saying that a wine with cork taint is not faulty if someone is happy to drink it. I will aim to be more objective, while recognizing that a degree of subjectivity is always involved when people taste wine.

THE STRUCTURE OF THIS BOOK

One by one, I will discuss each of the recognized wine faults. I'll try to keep these chapters practically focused, looking at how wine faults present themselves in the real world and giving advice on how they might be avoided. I'll also try to assess just how much of a threat or problem each of these faults is. Certain themes—those raised here in the discussion—are recurring. I considered whether to provide a reference for every statement, as in a scientific review, but that would make this book what it isn't—a book for wine scientists. So I decided to add references to a few of the most important studies and reviews, but this is by no means intended as a complete account of the literature. While I've made every effort to ensure accuracy, to have cited a peer-reviewed paper supporting each statement would have changed the nature of the book. In addition, there is often disagreement in the scientific literature on many of these topics, and to note each contrasting viewpoint would have been tedious. Instead, to produce what I believe is the most accurate account of each of the faults we are dealing with, I combined my reading of the literature with insights from winemakers' practical experience and my own knowledge of wine. The quotes included here are taken from conversations and interviews with winemakers and wine scientists. I travel extensively, and in the course of that travel I speak to many people: the individuals quoted here are just a subset of those I've discussed the subject of wine faults with. More of them could have been quoted, and I'm grateful to all who have taken time to talk openly with me and share their experience. They have all helped shape the content of this book, but ultimately I have had to form my own opinions. Therefore, this book is not completely neutral: it consists of the facts and of educated interpretations of the facts. I hope that it makes a useful addition to the wine literature, while being broad enough in scope to be of use across the wine trade.

CHAPTER TWO

The Chronology of
Wine Faults

Here I trace the various points in wine production where quality can be lost and faults introduced.

PLANTING A VINEYARD   The grape variety/rootstock choice needs to be appropriate for the site. Get this choice wrong and you could face loss of quality, for example from excessively high vigor (creating susceptibility to disease through bad airflow in the fruit zone, poor ripening of fruit, and difficulty in balancing phenolic and sugar ripeness), susceptibility to disease (some varieties don't like to be grown in damper climates), premature ripening (wine quality can be lost when harvest takes place in the heat of summer), or delayed ripening (quality can be lost by harvesting too late when the weather is poor). And factors such as row orientation and vine spacing also matter. Get it right, and you save yourself a lot of bother later on.

TRELLISING SYSTEM/VINE TRAINING   The right system must be applied for each combination of site and variety. Not every site suits a high-VSP (vertical shoot position) canopy.

In sunny climates, dappled shade provided by a single-wire umbrella sprawl (the way most Australian vineyards used to be trellised) or by bush vines works really well, protecting grapes from the heat of the sun. Big canopies can provide too much photosynthetic power and result in very high sugar levels by the time the grapes are phenolically ripe, leading to alcoholic wines that need lots of correction in the winery to stabilize. But at the same time, if the vine is over-vigorous, excessive growth of the canopy can cause shading of fruit and increase the risk of disease, and the grapes can have problems ripening.

IRRIGATION   Vines need water. Too much or too little and wine quality is affected. Great vineyard sites seem, in most seasons, to deliver just the right amount of water to the vine at the right time. Irrigation regimes can be tailored to do this too. But the presence of irrigation and the way in which it is used will influence the growth of vine roots and the canopy, which, in turn, will have an impact on wine quality.

CANOPY MANAGEMENT   The choice of how to manage the fruit zone is a critical one. Sometimes grapes need to be protected from the light, and removing the leaves in the fruit zone would be damaging. Often, though, getting rid of these leaves can reduce the risk of disease and enhance wine quality. A lot depends on the light environment, the ambient temperature, the row orientation (afternoon sun is warmer than morning sun), and the timing of leaf removal.

SPRAYING REGIMES AND CULTIVATION   Grape vines are susceptible to a number of pests and diseases, so appropriate sprays are needed to keep crops healthy. The timing and nature of these are critical if quality is not to be lost. Nutrients used up by the vine also need to be provided. Weeds need to be dealt with, chemically or by mechanical cultivation. This is a complicated topic, because while wanting to eradicate pests and diseases, enlightened winegrowers also want to preserve the ecological diversity of the vineyard agroecosystem. Inappropriate spraying can damage the microbial ecology of the vineyard and create a monoculture, with negative effects on wine quality. Microbial diseases of vines are directly responsible for some wine faults. Geosmin is a good example of this, as is enzymic oxidation of grape juice.

HARVESTING   Choosing when to pick is one of the key decisions in terms of wine quality. Pick too soon and you get unripe characters in the wine. Pick too late and you end up with low acidity, high sugar (thus high potential alcohol), and dead-fruit characters. If you delay picking and the weather turns, you risk rotten grapes and/or dilute wine. The choice of hand or machine harvest can also have quality implications, as can decisions about day versus night harvest in warm wine regions.

TRIAGE   Selecting which grapes to use, either by selective picking or using a triage table, is an important quality step. It's important to discard rotten grapes to avoid raising the risk of wine faults. These days there are increasingly sophisticated options available for sorting, ranging from the Mistral (which blows away raisined grapes and fragments of non-grape material) to the super-selective optical sorting devices. Another approach is to go through the vineyard removing rotten or unripe grapes by hand before picking the healthy grapes (for example, by machine).

PRESSING WHITE WINES   It's possible to lose quality at pressing. For example, for some white wines, oxygen must be avoided at this stage; for others, deliberate juice hyperoxidation is positive. If the wrong phenolics are left in the juice, the wine can be susceptible to oxidation later on.

CLARIFYING THE MUST   An important choice in winemaking is how clean the winemaker wants the must to be. Fermenting with high solids can increase the risk of reduction (caused by volatile sulfur compounds), but this can also be used to try to develop positive reductive characters in wine if that is desired. Also, the use of enzymes can speed settling of the juice if ferments with clear juice are desired. Flotation and centrifugation are now common means of clarifying the must, rather than just allowing the solids to settle.

MACERATING RED WINES   Overextraction, or clumsy extraction, is one way to lose quality in red wines, resulting in inappropriate bitterness or astringency. If the cap is not kept moist, acetic acid bacteria can create volatile acidity.

SULFUR DIOXIDE ADDITION   A major way of preventing unwanted microbial growth and avoiding oxidation, added sulfur is a major factor in helping produce fault-free wines. Timing and the quantity used are important. The choice to use less sulfur dioxide carries risks, but also the potential for quality gains; if this path is taken, great attention must be paid to what is going on with the wine.

PRIMARY FERMENTATION   If the primary fermentation starts too slowly, wine quality can be affected. For some wines, such as aromatic whites and lighter reds, fermentation at too high a temperature can result in loss of fruitiness. If the wrong "wild" yeasts dominate the first stages of fermentation, off-flavors can develop. If ferments stick, the wines can quickly turn volatile—

a major risk. If not all the sugar is used up, the risk of *Brettano-myces* is increased. There is also the risk of reduction, caused by the yeast's production of volatile sulfur compounds. Yeasts are critically important in wine quality.

MALOLACTIC FERMENTATION   The bacteria that carry out malolactic fermentation have a marked sensory impact on the wine. This can be both positive and negative. If the wrong strains carry it out, excessive diacetyl production is a risk or bio-genic amines can be formed in the wine. Bacterial fermentation is a critical issue in winemaking, and it's one that hasn't received enough attention.

WINE AGING AND STORAGE   Time spent in barrels comes with a number of risks. The first is the development of *Brett-anomyces* in red wines—one of the main worries of all red-wine makers. Then there's the risk of oxidation, which can occur in barrels that aren't kept properly topped up, or where *bâtonnage* (lees stirring) is excessive. Reduction can also develop in bar-rel. The choice of vessel for wine aging is important. Excessive oak could be considered a fault, as could the taste of terracotta if lower-quality amphoras are used. Poorly stored oak, too, can result in unwanted flavor.

BOTTLING   Excessive oxygen pickup during bottling can result in quality loss. The decision of whether to fine and/or filter the wine before bottling is also important for quality, as is the choice of closure. Natural cork carries with it a risk of cork taint and of greater variability between bottles of the same wine. The oxygen transmission rate of the closure will have a large impact on the way in which the wine develops after bottling.

STORAGE AND THE LOGISTICS CHAIN   There is huge potential for post-bottling quality loss through unsuitable environmental exposure to heat and light. Wines are frequently shipped at temperatures that can cause quality loss, and light exposure in the retail environment can also damage quality. For fine wines, cellaring conditions are important.

CHAPTER THREE

Brettanomyces

- **What is it?** A microbiological fault caused by a rogue yeast that's commonly found in red-wine maturation. It's also common in bottle-fermented sparkling wines, especially those made by the transfer method.
- **What is its flavor impact?** Affected wines show animal/spicy/phenolic characters and lose fruitiness, and they often develop a characteristic drying metallic sensation on the back palate.
- **What causes it?** *Brettanomyces bruxellensis,* a yeast whose growth is encouraged by high pH (because of its effects on sulfur dioxide efficacy), low sulfur dioxide, a bit of residual sugar, high turbidity, and warm cellars.
- **Is it always bad?** No. Some people like the flavor. A little bit can be a nice seasoning in the right context. The problem is, it is almost impossible to control.
- **How can it be prevented?** Good cellar hygiene, good sulfur dioxide management, cool cellars, minimal delay

between the end of alcoholic fermentation and the beginning of malolactic, low pH, no residual sugar in the wine, and sterile filtration. And good luck.
- **How common is it?** Really common. More common than most people realize.

We begin our exploration of wine faults with one of the most interesting, and also one of the most prevalent. It's *Brettanomyces,* commonly known as "brett," and this is largely a red-wine problem. Why is it so interesting? Because it's one of those faults that is sometimes not a fault. Whether or not it's a problem in a wine is dependent on the level, the context, and also the preferences of the drinker. Many of the world's great red wines have levels above threshold, although now that the wine world is more aware of brett—its strongly savory character often used to be attributed to terroir—it's fair to say that there are fewer winemakers happy to have it in their wines. It's also interesting because some of the practices used to minimize its presence are in conflict with winemaking approaches beneficial for quality.

Brettanomyces is a genus of yeast, also known as *Dekkera* (the yeast can exist in two states, and the latter name is used for the sexual, spore-producing form). While several species names are commonly used, the current classification has the wine-relevant *Brettanomyces* as just two species, *B. bruxellensis* and *B. anomala,* the former being by far the more important. In this chapter, we will refer to *Brettanomyces* by its nickname brett.

It wasn't until the early years of the twentieth century that brett was discovered, and that was by the brewing industry, not by winemakers. In brewing, it's an important yeast in making some traditional British and Belgian beer styles. When the first single-culture *Saccharomyces cerevisiae* yeasts (this is the species of yeast that carries out most of the alcoholic fermentation in wine) were used to make British beers, people noticed that something was missing: the imprint of brett, which in the context of the right beer can add real interest. It so happens that brewers commonly refer to brett character in beer as "vinous." Brewers can actually buy cultured brett—something that would horrify most winemakers! (As an aside, though, I know of a winemaker who has inoculated a wine with a brewer's cultured strain of brett because he appreciated the quality in Gewürztraminer—which, as a high-pH white variety, sometimes shows this character. The resulting wine was quite nice.)

Brett can be a huge problem for makers of red wine if the risk factors are not well managed. White wines are usually less at risk because of their lower pH and lower levels of suitable substrates. But brett can be a big problem in skin-fermented ("orange") white wines and is also reported to be an issue in sparkling wines. It is one of the most interesting of all wine faults, because many highly celebrated red styles contain levels of brett high enough for it to have some sensory impact. Some people think that if brett is detectable by a taster then the wine is faulty, but others quite like it (we'll discuss this later).

The reason brett is a particular problem is twofold. First of all, it is very prevalent, and if you create a wine in which brett can grow, it probably will do so. Second, it is an annoyingly resilient yeast—sitting around, biding its time, and then growing in conditions that virtually nothing else can grow in. In practical terms, this means that it does its real damage after the regular alcoholic fermentation is complete. Brett is slow-growing (although, given the right conditions, it can grow quite quickly) and doesn't need much to feed on. Its low nutritional requirements allow it to colonize harsh niches. Interestingly, although it is often taught that brett is hard to kill, the same dose of sulfur dioxide (SO_2) that will kill *Saccharomyces cerevisiae* will kill brett. The notion that brett is some sort of superbug that is hard to kill and control is not correct, although there are some reports of specific brett strains that are unusually resistant to SO_2. It seems that brett is highly adaptive and often finds ways of surviving.

It is now widely claimed that brett survives in what is known as a "viable but nonculturable" (VBNC) state. This state is common in bacteria but was only recently suggested to exist in eukaryotic cells such as yeasts. For brett, the first study highlighting its existence was published in 2012,[1] and a more recent paper characterized the VBNC behavior of seven strains of brett.[2] The idea is that the stress of a large dose of sulfites causes a range of changes in live brett cells that cause them to shut down much of their metabolism, which means that traditional microbiological attempts to look for brett miss it, even when it is present and waiting for a chance to grow again. And filters that catch live brett cells can miss any VBNC brett cells, which are smaller. But this is a controversial idea. Several research teams around the world have looked for VBNC in brett and failed to find it. According to Peter Godden of the Australian Wine Research Institute (AWRI),

The notion of VBNC with brett is inconsistent with observations of the control or total elimination of brett in many Australian wineries, over a period of ten years. If the VBNC state is real for brett, then it would be expected that at least some of the many wineries in Australia which have effectively eliminated it would be suffering from that phenomenon. However, the AWRI knows of none. Therefore, people who believe that the VBNC exists for brett need to explain why they claim it exists in some winemaking regions around the world and not others.

RECOGNIZING BRETT

Before we look in depth at the factors that contribute to brett problems, let's first focus on perhaps the most important bit: what are the key characteristics of this wine fault as it might be encountered in wine? The sensory effects of brett are many. The first sign is reduced varietal character, followed by the degradation of certain fruity aromas by esterases present in this yeast. Esterases are enzymes that cause the breakdown of esters, a chemical group important in conferring fruitiness. Thus, grape varieties such as Pinot Noir are particularly badly hit by brett, because the wine loses its bright cherry and violet characters; this loss of fruit can be an early sign of the presence of brett while the wine is in barrel. Brett also utilizes what are otherwise nonfermentable sugars. These are present at low levels in "dry" red wines and can contribute to the fruity character: you miss them when they are gone.

Next, hints of smoke and spice begin to appear, the chief culprit being a compound called 4-ethylguaiacol, or 4-EG. As the infection progresses, the wine will begin to smell and taste medicinal (4-ethylphenol, or 4-EP, is largely responsible for this), and it will lose its fruity flesh, exposing the structural bones of the wine. Typically, the acid and tannins will stick out a bit. Finally, the wine will begin to smell of barnyards, horses, animal sheds, and Band-Aids. The characteristic metallic sensation on the back palate that many people experience with brett is confirmation of its presence.

It's actually quite difficult to teach people how to spot brett, because the characteristics of bretty wines vary depending on the substrates that were initially available to the brett cells as they multiplied, the context of the other flavors present in the wine, and perhaps the precise strain of brett involved (although work by the

AWRI failed to identify differences among the genetically different Australian strains in their formation of aroma active compounds). Depending on the combination of spoilage compounds produced and their relative concentrations, the overall effects of brett will differ. Some bretty wines show more earthy and spicy; others are more at the fecal/barnyard end of the spectrum. The aromas associated with brett:

· Band-Aid
· medicinal
· Germolene antiseptic cream
· pharmaceutical
· barnyard-like
· animal
· horsey
· sweaty
· leathery
· mouse urine
· wet dog
· smoky
· spicy
· cheesy
· rancid
· metallic

THE PREVALENCE OF BRETT

Brett appears to be quite common in red wines. It is less frequently found in whites for a few reasons, including the lower pH that whites typically have. Low pH protects against brett because it makes any SO_2 present much more effective. Wine scientist Pascal Chatonnet, who was responsible for much of the ground-breaking research on this subject, surveyed the incidence of brett in a variety of red wines some years ago and found that just under a third had levels of 4-EP above 600 μg/L. Used as a diagnostic indicator for the presence of brett, 4-EP is found only in wines that have a brett infection. Most people can spot it at around 420 μg/L, but this will vary with the style of wine and the sensitivity of individual tasters. It would be better to say that the threshold ranges from 300 to 600 μg/L, depending on wine style.

Chatonnet and colleagues[3] compared the ability of brett to synthesize volatile phenols from their precursors *trans-p-*coumaric and ferulic acids and compared this with lactic acid bacteria and *Saccharomyces cerevisiae*. Neither *S. cerevisiae* nor the lactic acid bacteria synthesized significant quantities of volatile phenols, confirming that brett is responsible for the development of a phenolic character in red wines. They also showed that brett is able to ferment the small quantities of residual sugars (glucose, fructose, galactose, and trehalose) in wine and that fermentation of 275 mg/L of these sugars (less than the normal residual sugar level of red wine at the end of fermentation) is enough to produce a level of ethylphenols that will alter the aromatics of the wine.

For his Master of Wine dissertation, Sam Harrop did a study in which he presented twenty-five of the world's leading Syrah-based wines in a blind tasting and asked those present to comment on whether they detected brett or not. He then sent away samples of the same wines to be chemically analyzed for 4-EP. A striking number of these wines showed above-threshold levels, including some famous names. A further clue to the extent of this problem is shown by data from the International Wine Challenge, the world's largest blind tasting, where brett consistently makes up around a third of all wine faults (typically, some fifteen thousand bottles of wine are tasted each year and 5–7 percent are deemed faulty). Indeed, over the past three years brett has shown signs of being an increasing problem, as Chatonnet has suggested.

THE VIABLE BUT NONCULTURABLE STATE

Perhaps one of the reasons brett can be such a problem is that it can enter the VBNC state.[4] As mentioned earlier, this is well known for bacteria but quite controversial for yeast cells such as brett. The traditional way of looking for microbes in wine is by culturing them on nutrient agar plates and then counting the colonies. But a technique called *direct epifluorescence* can give rather different results, because it shows that some of the cells are alive but not capable of dividing. If a wine is sulfited, there is a massive reduction in the lactic acid bacteria and acetic acid bacteria seen by the plating technique. But direct epifluorescence shows that there is still a viable population: cells that have entered the VBNC state. A recent study showed that brett can also switch to the VBNC state when it is hit with a dose of sulfur dioxide[5], and these VBNC cells are a lot smaller than the actively growing ones. This means that they can now get through filters that otherwise would have trapped them. Brett cells are normally 5–8 × 3–4 μm, but this study showed that the VBNC cells are 22 percent smaller. The study showed that brett became nonculturable after two days in response to sodium metabisulfite addition but remained viable. Stressor removal by pH modification in the growth medium allowed the VBNC cells to exit the nonculturable state, thus demonstrating the resuscitation ability of brett VBNC cells for the first time. Attempts to replicate this experiment have been made but have largely failed. So, although this is a very attractive idea, it's one we have to treat quite cautiously for now.

Brett has been shown, in research by Renouf and colleagues, to possess the ability to survive in wine after bottling.[6] They examined the effectiveness of various filtration regimes in removing brett, finding—as you would expect—that the smaller the pore size, the more microbes were eliminated. Elimination of yeasts required a 1 μm filter, and elimination of bacteria required a 0.3 μm filter. After a number of years in bottle, volatile phenol concentrations were lower in more tightly filtered wines.

HOW IT HAPPENS, AND WHY IT IS INCREASING (AT LEAST IN SOME PARTS OF THE WORLD)

The risk factors for brett are several. When I asked New Zealand consultant winemaker Matt Thomson about the risk factors for brett, he said:

> If you have more new oak in your cellar, you will get more brett. If you have high-pH wines, and harvest riper, you will get more brett. If you harvest riper and end up with high brix, the ferments will struggle towards the end and you'll get more brett. If you go to barrel with some residual sugar, you will get more brett. If you have low SO_2 or leave the wine with no SO_2 after malolactic fermentation for an extended time, you will get more brett. If you adopt practices that allow cross-contamination of barrels, you will get more brett. If you have a warm cellar you will have more brett. If you do these things that promote brett, brett will become a bigger problem.

TABLE 1

Percentage of SO_2 in the Molecular Form
at Different pH Levels

pH	Molecular SO_2
2.9	7.5
3.0	6.1
3.1	4.9
3.2	3.9
3.3	3.1
3.4	2.5
3.5	2.0
3.6	1.6
3.7	1.3
3.8	1.0
3.9	0.8

High pH is a huge risk factor for brett. This is because at higher pH, much less SO_2 is going to be present in the molecular form, which is the active form of this molecule. You can see in table 1 how significant the effect of pH is.

Higher cellar temperature is another risk factor. In a paper published in 2013, Zuehlke and Edwards examined the relationship between culturability/viability of brett and temperature and molecular SO_2 levels.[7] While it is widely understood that the presence of adequate levels of molecular SO_2 protects against brett, there is also evidence that cold cellars are protective and may lessen the requirement for SO_2. Zuehlke and Edwards looked at four molecular SO_2 (mSO_2) concentrations (0.0, 0.2, 0.5, and 1.1

mg/L) and four storage temperatures (22°C, 18°C, 15°C, and 10°C). Just one strain of brett regained culturability following exposure to 0.5 mg/L mSO_2 at 18°C, and only one strain (a different one) remained culturable in the absence of mSO_2 at 10°C. The brett strains regained the ability to be cultured regardless of the concentration of mSO_2 present. These results support the idea that *Brettanomyces* can enter a VBNC state on exposure to sulfites—which means that cool cellars and adequate mSO_2 will limit spoilage by Brett but won't eradicate it.

Higher alcohol levels are a risk factor for brett. First of all, grapes picked late tend to have high pH, and significant quantities of tartaric acid are often needed to correct this. More directly, higher-alcohol wines are at risk because as alcohol rises, the yeasts struggle, with the result that sometimes a bit of sugar is left unfermented.

The use of wood cooperage is a risk factor, because the staves of barrels can harbor residual populations of brett that are very hard to remove. Brett can be found as far as 8 mm into staves, which makes it almost impossible to completely sterilize barrels using steam—a surface treatment, which might make things worse by damaging the wood surface. Ozone is also a surface treatment. The most effective treatment is radiated heat, such as filling the barrel with very hot water for a few hours. Interestingly, new oak also seems to be a risk factor (as Matt Thomson alludes to above), even though most people assume it is dirty old barrels that cause the problem. Thomson thinks that some cooperages, in his experience, produce new barrels that are more likely to cause brett problems. He won't name names, though. He says:

I'd love some research to be done on coopers and brett. Coopers understandably run a mile if you mention it. Think about the very specific metabolism that *Brettanomyces* has. It can use oak lactones. The chances of *Brettanomyces* evolving in the absence of those substrates and having that ability to metabolize those specific substrates would be pretty low. It would be a huge coincidence. The chances are that they have grown up in the presence of oak in forests....

If someone went and had a decent look for *Brettanomyces* in the forests in France, they might find that it is there. If you swab the inside surface of a toasted barrel, of course you won't find it. But if you split the barrel apart and look between the staves where wine leaches in and then leaches out, you'll probably find it. I think there's a decent chance that Brett is resident in perhaps some forests. Brett didn't appear to be there in the 1980s. I think the boom in oak usage that occurred because Robert Parker said oak is good and let's have more meant that the coopers expanded. They probably started recruiting forests that may have had high levels of brett. That is my theory, and I'd love someone to do the research to find out whether this is the case....

Because we stopped the cross-contamination—and we are pretty rigorous on that—we have found that some coopers tend to have more brett, some where every barrel has brett, and some that don't seem to have brett. We have concluded that the bretty barrels either come with brett, or the oak promotes brett to a greater extent by having more substrates. We can't rule either out. It warrants research.

WINERY CLEANLINESS

If you create conditions in the wine that suit brett growth, will it grow? Or is it a combination of the inoculum—brett actually present—plus the conditions in the wine? Some people talk of having a brett contamination in the winery as if it were a very rare inoculum of brett, such as one barrel with it, while others seem to think that all you need to do to get brett is to create conditions favorable for it. Which is the truth? "If you don't clean the winery properly you are leaving a lot of grot all over the place," says Adrian Coulter of the AWRI, "and you have substrate for growth. If your wine is continually getting exposed to oxygen, yeasts love oxygen and it kicks them off a bit more each time the wine is exposed. If you are topping your barrels every week you are letting in more air." He thinks this could encourage brett growth, as well as increasing the risk for volatile acidity.

California wine technologist and winemaker Clark Smith has an interesting idea about brett. He refers to it as a "hospital infection." According to his view, brett is less likely to be a problem if the wine has a healthy ecosystem of microbes, even if very little SO_2 is used. But create a wine with limited populations of microbes, and brett is freer to grow. One related idea is that if a wild ferment takes place, with lots of species of microbes participating at different times, this diversity will result in a wider spectrum of nutrients being consumed, leaving less for brett to feed on later in the winemaking process.

> **Turbidity** is a risk factor, and it helps to rack carefully to have no solids present in the aging wine. "You can have wines with low total sulfur dioxide but the ratio of free to bound is excellent because the turbidity is low," says Coulter. He recalls working with a large winery where it proved harder than normal to eradicate brett. "We got the wines down to analyze and they were pretty turbid," he recalls. "Whatever was causing the turbidity was binding up the sulfur dioxide. Potentially, if you have turbidity you have substrates that brett can metabolize."

Stuck and sluggish fermentations open the door to brett growth, so it's helpful to make sure ferments complete promptly and finish nicely. Using the right yeasts, or the right combination of yeasts, might help here. Watching fermentation temperatures and dynamics is advisable. It's important not to temperature-shock yeasts when pressing red wines, especially if whole-bunch ferments are used at all. This is because pressing releases some sugars from any whole berries left in the ferment, and you want the yeasts to carry on and ferment those sugars, lest they become ideal food for brett and other spoilage organisms.

Vineyard sources of brett contamination need to be considered. Some winemakers have identified specific vineyard sources that always seem to cause problems with brett in their cellars. This subject hasn't been well researched, but there are suggestions that significant populations of brett are present on grapes. Some estimates are that half of incoming grapes have some brett on them, especially for vineyards near roads, with a lot of wind, with earth movement, or with clusters close to the ground.[8] Bill Downie, who makes wine in a very natural way in The Gippsland region of Victoria, Australia, is convinced that vineyard management is a key factor in brett, and that good vineyard management with a healthy microbial ecology is protective. This is an interesting idea, and it would be interesting to pursue it scientifically. A New Zealand winemaker who deals with lots of growers shared this view with me: that certain vineyard blocks consistently carry with them higher risk of brett. "There's been talk about it endlessly," says Peter Godden of the AWRI. "Brett is ubiquitous. It's in the winery; it's probably in the vineyard, but no one has been able to prove this categorically."

AVOIDING BRETT

What can be done to avoid brett? This is where things get really interesting, because many of the steps needed to ensure clean wines run counter to the sort of winemaking approach you'd want to take to make *interesting* wines.

The first is to avoid barrels. Stainless steel can be cleaned properly, which vastly reduces the risk. Second, you need to avoid cross-contamination. When taking barrel samples, Matt Thomson uses plastic "barrel thieves" that are used just once and then sterilized. He also avoids doing "rack-and-return," where the wine would go from several barrels to be mixed up in one tank: instead, each barrel is racked separately to tank and returned, and the tank is cleaned before the procedure is repeated with the next barrel. I don't know of many winemakers who are this careful.

The next stage is to keep pH low, either by acidifying or harvesting earlier. This is very helpful in the fight against brett (although in Australia over the past thirty years, pH in wine has gone up while brett has fallen markedly, because winemakers have appreciated the brett risks of higher pH and have acted accordingly). Because brett is so widespread, you want to make your wine an uninviting habitat for its growth. To put it the other way, if you make your wine the sort of place where brett is happy growing, it will. Low pH is important for two reasons. First, brett doesn't like more acidic media because any SO_2 additions will be much more effective at lower pH, and more of the

SO_2 will be in the active molecular form (see table 1). Timing of SO_2 addition is also important. It is best to add it in large doses at the right time, rather than little by little. This results in a better ratio of free to total SO_2. When added in dribbles, it tends to get bound, and less is then present in the free form. By following this advice, Australian winemakers saw their ratio of free to bound rise from 0.30 to 0.45, resulting in cleaner wines. Research by the AWRI has shown that strains of brett differ threefold in their tolerance to SO_2.[9]

Another important preventive measure is to keep the time from the end of alcoholic fermentation to the end of malolactic fermentation as short as possible. Sulfur dioxide levels have to be kept low in order to facilitate the malolactic fermentation, which makes this a risky time in terms of potential brett growth. Therefore, inoculating for malolactic fermentation is advisable—and then, after that's complete, it's a good idea to add a whack of SO_2 to protect the wine for the rest of its time in barrel or tank. For inexpensive reds, co-inoculating with specific strains of yeast and bacteria so that malolactic takes place alongside primary fermentation is an effective strategy, resulting in very attractive fruit-forward wines.

Other preventive steps include avoiding lees aging, keeping barrels topped up, keeping cellar temperatures low (this is an important protective factor), avoiding temperature changes, and aggressively cleaning new and used barrels (it's impossible to clean a barrel completely, but filling it with very hot water for a period is effective).

The AWRI's *Brettanomyces* program has shown that with the right information and practices, winegrowers can reduce the risk of brett substantially. They instituted an eight-point protocol for reducing brett. This included focusing on pH and SO_2 use, temperature, getting through malolactic fermentation quickly, avoiding leaving brett substrates in the wine, and fermenting through to dryness. Largely because of the AWRI's brett initiative, the mean level of 4-EP in Australian Cabernet Sauvignon dropped from over 1,000 μg/L in 2000 to 107 μg/L in the 2005 vintage (the threshold for detection is 300–600 μg/L, depending on wine style). In the 2006 vintage, 21 percent of wines had "nondetectable" levels of 4-EP or 4-EG.

"We stopped the brett survey of bottled wine eight years ago," says Peter Godden of the AWRI. "We were getting a large proportion of wines with nondetectable 4-EP." He explains the strategy they took: "We started off with what we called the six brettiest wineries across the country, which included a couple of high-profile wineries. Two or three years later they'd have been the last places you'd go to if you wanted to isolate brett cells. This was just with good management throughout the winery." He cites a winery in Victoria where they had built a new temperature-controlled barrel warehouse. "That's when their brett problem really kicked off," he recalls. "It was just one or two degrees warmer than the old cellar across the road, but the same wines in the same sort of barrels in the new shed suddenly started turning bretty."

Godden points out that the Australian wine shows are a good source of data and demonstrate how much progress has been made with faults: "I'd say the level of faults is minimal [compared] to, say, ten or twenty years ago. With brett there are bretty barrels and bretty wines out there, but they don't end up in bottle any more. People are getting on top of brett." Adrian Coulter agrees: "It has gone down massively, but it is still bubbling along. People are talking about it. They might not put it into bottle; they might put it through reverse osmosis and blend. So it is not getting out into the market."

CURING BRETT

If brett has been at work on a wine, there are two ways that a winemaker can deal with the problem. One is to remove the volatile phenols that brett has produced. The other is to eliminate the brett cells. Sometimes both approaches are needed.

How can volatile phenols be removed? One way is to use absorbents such as PVPP (at 60–480 mg/L) or activated charcoal (15–240 mg/L), both of which have been reported to lower ethylphenol levels. However, other reports suggest that this makes little difference, so the jury is out.

Another approach is to use yeasts. *Saccharomyces cerevisiae* is an efficient biosorbent and can absorb volatile phenols such as 4-EP.[10] However, the sorption capacity of 4-EP by yeasts is greatly influenced by strain, methods of drying the yeast, the medium used for yeast biomass production, and drying after harvesting. Interestingly, active dried yeasts are better at it than yeasts that haven't been through the industrial drying process. Sorption of 4-EP occurs at the surface of the yeast wall, and in a model wine it was possible to remove a third of volatile phenols. It may be that using inactivated dried yeasts, which are now available as enological products, could take out a proportion of volatile phenols, reducing their sensory impact in wine. This could be a good approach because it has less effect on the color and quality of red wine than other methods.

Removing brett itself is quite challenging. One way is to fine red wines before putting them in barrel. Populations of brett can be reduced by 40- to 2,000-fold by treatment with fining proteins. The more fining that takes place, the more brett is reduced, and also fining with casein or potassium caseinate can reduce ethylphenol levels. The problem with fining like this is that it is not specific and also reduces wine aroma and color.

Filtration is effective. However, the pore size needs to be as small as 0.45 μm, and this damages the wine's colloidal structure, thereby affecting its texture.

Another method is to use a chemical called DMDC (dimethyl dicarbonate, also known by its trade name Velcorin), which is extremely toxic to microbes but breaks down into harmless products once it has done its job. The wine will still have the impact of the compounds associated with brett, but at least it won't get any worse and will be stable in bottle.

Finally, there is a promising new solution: chitosan.[11] This is a biopolymer produced by the deacetylation of chitin, and it has already been used as a microbicide in applications such as food preservation and wound dressing. Its microbiological activity depends on factors such as its molecular weight and degree of deacetylation (there is more than one chitosan, chemically speaking). The type of chitosan used in wine is derived from the fungus *Aspergillus niger* and is produced by the KitoZyme company. It was approved for use in wine in 2010 by the International Organisation of Vine and Wine, and at a dosage of 4 g/hL it has been shown to eliminate brett in a real-wine scenario. The mechanism of action was unknown for several years, but it is now thought to be through adsorption of brett cells onto the polymer through electrostatic forces, which changes the cell wall's structure and permeability.[12] This product is now available commercially as No Brett Inside or KiOfine-B. While it seems to be effective in removing brett, it has no effect on any volatile phenols already present in the wine.

IS BRETT ALWAYS A PROBLEM?

So now we come to a thorny question: Is brett always a problem, or are there contexts in which it is OK? If you were a winemaker, you'd probably want to avoid it altogether because it is so difficult to control. But, perhaps through luck, some wines seem to work even though they have noticeable brett. Unlike many other wine faults, which are more clear-cut, it becomes a matter of personal preference. Wines that seem to successfully carry brett are often those from warmer climates, where the sweetness of the fruit seems to be complemented quite well by the earthy, spicy funk of brett. Yet there will be some people who find brett objectionable no matter what the context. This makes brett a problematic wine "fault" when it comes to restaurant service. If a sommelier tries a wine and finds some brett, should they point it out to the customer? Probably not, because the customer may find the wine to be perfectly acceptable. If, however, a customer refuses a wine because it is bretty, then in this context the wine is faulty. Perhaps, to avoid such problems, sommeliers should warn customers of the implications of ordering wines from producers whose house style is known to include a significant flavor imprint of brett.

Brett is something that the trade needs to become more aware of. "Lots of winemakers still haven't grasped the complexity of *Brettanomyces*," says Matt Thomson, "and there's still a bit of denial out there." It's also something that he thinks everyone can get. "All decent tasters can pick the nuances of brett once you tune into it."

Some people seem to like brett, though. "It is a generational thing," says Michael Hill Smith of Australian winery Shaw and Smith,

The older tasters—the old guard—got brought up with brett in wines which I think they felt was part of the style. People got used to it, and didn't realize that it was a flaw. Then you have the new guard, who understand it and recognize it. The old guys just don't get it because it wasn't part of their learning experience.

According to Hill Smith, "The mistake people are making is that they have tasted many good and great old wines that happened to have a little bit of brett. But they are great wines in spite of the brett, and normally it is a small amount." He doesn't much care for it:

> I don't have a major problem with a small amount of brett on the nose, but as soon as it is on the palate and it strips fruit, it is such a negative. It is a time bomb in bottle; you buy a wine in good faith and ten years later not only does it have a brett aroma, it has a stripped fruit palate. I don't want brett in any of my wines, and I don't want brett in any of the wines I am buying. I have a cellar of old Bordeaux through the period where there was a lot of brett and it is disappointing.

Some varieties do better with brett than others. Cabernet- and Merlot-based wines seem to handle brett quite well. Pinot Noir and Nebbiolo less so. But opinions are divided. Matt Donaldson, winemaker at Pegasus Bay in New Zealand's Waipara region, is a little sympathetic to brett, even in Pinot. "There's a hint of brett in the [Pegasus Bay] 2011 Pinot Noir," he says.

> I really like a little bit of brett, but I don't want it to dominate the wine. The difference between New World Pinot Noir and Burgundy is, I think, brett. There's more brett in good-quality Burgundy than people realize. Most of the good producers are on to it and are making sure that it doesn't dominate the wine. I think it's a vineyard thing, to some extent, so with some vineyards we always add sulfur. You only want a bit of it for Pinot Noir, but for Merlot

and Cabernet, the more brett the better for me. In Bordeaux, brett never seems to dominate. It seems to fit a lot better. Our best years for Bordeaux-style wines is when they have a pH approaching four, when they have mouthfeel and brett.

Matt Thomson disagrees about Pinot:

There was some research some time ago that showed that 4-EG is produced at much higher levels in Pinot Noir than 4-EP is. This is what I find: I tend to get the medicinal, smoky, 4-EG notes more than I do 4-EP. If you have 4-EP in a Pinot it is well gone. It is hugely bretty. I find 4-EG quite disturbing to be honest, because the other thing that has gone on is that you have lost your pentose and your body, and more importantly you have lost the fruit.

Thomson suggests that brett takes away the nonfermentable sugars that would otherwise add a bit of rounded character to the wine:

Brett does metabolize the pentoses, and at low levels of residual sugar (2–4 g/L) you don't pick sweetness, but you pick body. Brett can take it from 1.5 g/L, which is bone dry as far as we can see it, and it can end up at 0.5. That 1 g will make a difference. The tannins look a bit more rustic. For me, with brett in Pinot and Nebbiolo, what disturbs me most is the loss. It is not what it adds, but what it takes away from those aromatic reds that really upsets me.

He adds, "It upsets me when I hear people say that a little bit of brett is OK in Pinot Noir. I think, obviously you don't know what it is like without it, or you wouldn't say that. It takes the magic away." He isn't so opposed to brett in wines made from the red Bordeaux varieties, though:

I think if you try a totally brett-free Merlot or Cabernet or blend [of them], you get fruit and oak, and there is a hole in the middle where there is nothing. Somehow the brett can fill that, and you get a

TABLE 2

Some Compounds Produced by *Brettanomyces*

Compound	Sensory impact
4-Ethylphenol	Band-Aid, medicinal, phenolic, horsey
4-Ethylguaiacol	Spicy, smoky, phenolic, cloves
Isovaleric acid	Sweaty, rancid, cheesey
4-Ethylcatechol	Medicinal, stables
2-Phenylethanol	Honey, spice, lilac
Guaiacol	Smoky
Ethyldecanoate	Fruity, appley, waxy
Trans-2-nonenal	Green, fatty
Isoamyl alcohol	Unpleasant
Ethyl-2-methylbutyrate	Fruity, peachy, appley

seamless flavor that goes right through. Is it a good thing? For me, it probably is, but as soon as that brett starts to extend above the level of the fruit and oak, it starts to be a problem and I am offended by it. You get this rustic note. To me, it is a matter of degree. For the Bordelaise, I think 1990 was their worst year for brett. They had a really ripe year, and on the back of some good vintages they used their money to buy barrels. In 1990, a big ripe year and lots of new oak culminated in massive brett levels. Since then the Bordelaise have been onto it, and if you look at the better châteaux now they have some brett but it is at a nice balanced level. They have really addressed it.

Pascal Chatonnet recognized that there was more brett in riper Bordeaux vintages. He suggests that this is because the grapes were picked earlier, and then the first post-malolactic racking always took place at the same time, after the New Year's break. Thus, the wine had been sitting for longer on lees without SO_2.

Brett is such an interesting topic. It's a fault, yet it's an accepted element of some fine wines, particularly those with age. It's a superb example of why we should take a more nuanced view of wine faults, rather than a binary "fault or no fault" view. In any case, brett is here to stay and winemakers need to be in control of it. I'll leave the closing comment to Peter Godden: "Brett is fantastic at finding its niche and evolving."

CHAPTER FOUR

Oxidation

- **What is it?** Loss of quality when wine comes into contact with excess oxygen.
- **What is its flavor impact?** It varies, from a slight lessening of fruitiness to more serious cases where fruit disappears and savory, earthy, spicy, bruised-apple characters dominate. It often co-occurs with other problems, such as volatile acidity and *Brettanomyces*.
- **What causes it?** Reactions taking place when oxygen comes into contact with wine components in the presence of phenolic compounds and transition metal ions. Inappropriate exposure of wines to air.
- **Is it always bad?** No. A degree of oxygen exposure at the right stage in winemaking is helpful. And some wine styles have slight or even total oxidation as part of the equation.
- **How can it be prevented?** By understanding the negative effects of oxygen and preventing the wine from coming into contact with air at the wrong stages.

- **How common is it?** Loss of quality through poor oxygen management is very common. Outright oxidation is rarer. Oxygen management is one of the most vital aspects of winemaking.

Oxidation is, like *Brettanomyces*, one of those faults that can divide people. Take an old Viña Tondonia Rioja Blanco and present it to your average New World winemaker, and they may well recoil in horror, declaring it oxidized. (I did this very recently with a couple of winemakers from New Zealand and Australia. Towards the end of the bottle they began to appreciate it. It was a close thing, though.) But we know serious wine people who love these wines (the author included), including most Spanish wine experts. All wines are exposed to oxygen at one stage or another, but it is when the exposure has been too great at the wrong stage, or is inappropriate for the wine style, that we have a problem.

But there's more to oxygen's role in wine than just the "fault" oxidation. Oxygen interacts with wine in complex ways, and poor oxygen management can cause a loss of quality, even if the wine isn't oxidized. So we need to regard oxygen both as a potential threat and as a winemaking tool. This chapter will deal with the topic of oxygen in two ways. First, the mechanism: what's going on in chemical terms? Second, the phenomenology: what happens to the character of wine that has experienced oxygen exposure?

It would be fair to say that oxygen management is probably the most important factor in wine quality, so we'll spend quite a bit of time on this subject. I would add, though, that the exact mechanisms of chemical oxidation of wine are still not completely understood, and there are multiple theories to explain the chemistry at this point. This is a somewhat controversial field.

THE MECHANISMS OF OXIDATION

Enzymic Oxidation

The first step in exploring the mechanisms of oxidation is to split it into two types: enzymic and nonenzymic (i.e., chemical) oxidation. Enzymes are proteins that make chemical reactions proceed more quickly—and, in some cases, make them more likely to happen—by a process called *catalysis*. They are really important biological molecules; for example, some drugs are enzymes. The usual way they work is that their three-dimensional structure brings molecules together, making a reaction between them more likely to happen. If you cut an apple open and leave the cut surface in contact with air, it will brown. This is an example of enzymic oxidation in action. Just as in the case of browning in apples, there is an enzyme present in grape must that's a polyphenol oxidase (PPO), specifically tyrosinase. In the presence of oxygen and tissue disruption, tyrosinase will cause the oxidation of phenols (we'll come to these important wine molecules in detail later) and the browning of the juice (if it's a white wine this is much more evident). Interestingly, the brown/black color of tea leaves is caused by the action of PPO in the processing of the leaves, so it can be useful in some situations. There's also a version of PPO produced by microbes, called *laccase*, which does the same thing and is harder to inactivate with sulfur dioxide than tyrosinase. So any grapes with a fungal rot such as botrytis will produce musts especially active in enzymic oxidation.

In white-wine making, there are two options with must handling, and both have their benefits and drawbacks. One is to protect the must from oxygen as much as possible, and the other is to deliberately allow exposure to oxygen at an early stage. This choice is all about what you want to happen with the phenolics in your wine. As we'll discuss in more detail later, there are two types of phenolic compounds in white wine. The first are the acid phenols, or more technically the *non-flavonoid phenolics*. These include cinnamic and benzoic acids, the main group being the hydroxycinnamic acids. These are found in the pulp of the grape. The second type is the *flavonoid phenolics*, which include what we refer to as "tannins" (procyanidins or proanthocyanidins or condensed tannins—they are all the same thing), anthocyanins (the pigments; white grapes don't have these), and compounds such as catechin and epicatechin. These are found mainly in the grape skin, but some of them come from the seed. How much of these you get in your must depends on how gently you press, but it will also depend on the quantities present in the grapes and the state of the grapes at harvest. Typically, lighter pressings will have fewer phenolics and the later press fractions will have more.

So white-wine makers looking to make very fruity, bright wines might decide to work reductively. They'll aim to press as gently as possible and avoid extended contact between the must and the skins; they will add sulfur dioxide at crushing (25–50 mg/L of sulfur dioxide should deactivate PPOs, but this will depend on the pH—more on this later); they may use fining agents (such as polyvinylpolypyrrolidone, potassium caseinate, activated charcoal, or chitosans) to remove any phenolics present; and they will try to keep air away from the must. Indeed, there are now presses on the market that use inert gas to make pressing totally anaerobic. One example is Bucher Vaslin's Inertys system, in which a big, flexible bag containing nitrogen gas is attached to the press. It breathes in and out like a lung, depending on the pressing phase. This creates a closed loop in which the gas is nitrogen, not air, protecting the juice from any oxidation at all. Of course, you could just inject nitrogen into the press with every cycling, but then you'd use a lot of it and the cost would be prohibitive. The creation of the closed loop is the key to the success of Inertys. This sort of reductive approach to must handling, when coupled with appropriate winemaking steps, preserves fruity flavor compounds such as thiols, which might otherwise be oxidized. But this will also prevent any phenolics in the juice from being oxidized, resulting in a wine that's highly susceptible to later oxygen exposure but that retains complex fruity flavors.

Glutathione, a sulfur-containing tripeptide, is an important player here. Its concentration in grape must varies, and it's an effective antioxidant because it is able to trap the quinones (once again, we'll come to these later—such is the complexity of this process that we'll be coming to a lot of things later) produced during the enzymic oxidation of must and prevent them from doing any damage. It specifically acts to prevent the loss of sulfur-containing compounds, such as the fruity thiols mentioned above. One of the reasons for protecting the must from oxygen during pressing is to prevent all the glutathione from being used up in this way, because glutathione is thought to be protective at later stages in the wine's life.

The contrasting approach is to allow enzymic oxidation of the must, avoiding these protective stages. In this scenario, you don't worry about must phenolics or sulfur dioxide additions. You just let PPO do its thing in a process known as "must hyperoxidation."[1] The juice turns a worrying brown color, but the brown phenolics precipitate out; and then, after fermentation is complete, the wine is much less susceptible to chemical oxidation and browning. However, this oxidative process also damages and removes many other flavor molecules, so it is sometimes avoided when these flavors are the goal.

Reductive winemaking creates wines that can be vulnerable to any oxygen later in their lives, such as after bottling. In both scenarios the idea is to lower the level of phenolics in the final wine—one by pressing delicately to avoid their presence in the first place, the other by oxidizing them before fermentation—because, as we will see later, phenolics are important players in chemical oxidation. For red wines things are quite different. This is because phenolic compounds have two sides to them as far as oxygen is concerned. They are players in the chemical oxidation process, but they also protect against oxidation because they can scavenge free radicals (specific chemicals that are also baddies when it comes to oxidation) and thus play a protective role. Red wines with a high concentration of phenolic compounds are protected from oxidation, but white wines with high phenolics are more at risk, because this "high" level in white wines is much lower than the "high" level in reds. How confusing is this? Some people think that harder pressing of white wines and skin contact, resulting in higher levels of flavonoid phenols (such as tannins) can actually be protective. In fact, in the distant past, before metal tanks were available, whites were deliberately made with more skin contact (called "orange wines") specifically to improve longevity in non-hermetic storage containers (wooden barrels or clay amphoras). It is clearly a complex situation, and because of its importance for wine quality, we'll need to explore this in more detail.

Chemical Oxidation

You probably won't be pleased to hear that the mechanisms of chemical oxidation are really complicated. That's the bad news. The good news is that I will try to explain them clearly in ways that won't make you fall asleep, keeping the chemical jargon to a minimum. I'll start by using an analogy, casting the elements involved as characters in a play.

The main character is named *oxygen*. He's not such a bad guy, when you catch him on his own. If fact, without his partners, it is impossible for him to react with wine! He can be quite useful and has an important role to play in the development of wine, especially at the early stages and especially with reds. But when oxygen gets together with two of his bad associates—that's when we have a problem. It transforms him into a dangerous character capable of causing a lot of damage. When he's hanging out with these guys, it's best if he's kept away from your wine.

The first of these dangerous characters is called *iron*. Iron turns oxygen mad, transforming him from a fairly harmless guy into a highly dangerous one. The second is a chap called *phenolics*. Oxygen, made mad by iron, transforms phenolics into his bad alter ego, *quinones*. And then iron gets involved again and makes oxygen even madder, and he just starts causing havoc.

Let's describe this scenario in chemical terms. The first player, oxygen, will be familiar to you: it's a gas, it forms 21 percent of the atmosphere, and we rely on it to breathe. We use it in respiration, the process of chemical reactions by which we break down food to create ATP, the currency of energy in our bodies. But oxygen can be dangerous, so our cells need compounds called *antioxidants* to protect valuable bits from the bad effects of oxygen, ensuring that oxygen only does the job it's supposed to do.

Technically, *oxidation* is defined as the gain of electrons by an oxidizing agent, and oxygen is very good at gaining electrons. In fact, oxygen's value to us is in the energy available from this process, which fuels our bodies and our cars. Perhaps the most striking illustration of this is fire: when oxygen gains a lot of electrons very rapidly, the heat and light energy of a flame result. Conversely, reduction is the loss of electrons.

So why is wine oxidation so complex? It's because of all the different players and the roles they play. Oxygen itself isn't terribly reactive when it comes into contact with wine, and for oxidation reactions to take place, it first needs to be made reactive. This is where the second player comes in: the transition metal ion, usually iron, which has the chemical symbol Fe (the ion is Fe^{2+}). The other transition metal that's worth noting is copper (Cu^{2+}), and the role of these ions is so crucial that wine scientist and expert on oxidation Dr. Andrew Waterhouse has gone so far to say, "If you would remove all iron and copper, all oxidation of wine would stop."

So this is the first stage in wine oxidation. Oxygen (O_2) reacts with iron (Fe^{2+}) ions to release radicals. In this reaction the Fe^{2+} becomes Fe^{3+}, while O_2 becomes HO-O, the hydroperoxyl radical. Free radicals like this are very reactive because they have an unpaired valence electron—a "dangling" bond. They are, in effect, highly reactive short-lived fragments of molecules capable of causing chemical havoc.

What does the hydroperoxyl radical do? This is where the third participant enters the story: the phenolic compounds in wine. Phenolic compounds such as catechol are vital players in the oxidation process, but their role is quite a confusing one. If we are going to get to grips with oxidation in wine, we will need to learn a little about phenolic compounds. This is a diversion in the story, but an important one.

Phenolic Compounds in Wine

Polyphenols are a large group of compounds that use a chemical structure called *phenol* as the basic building block; they are *poly*phenols because more than one phenol group is joined to another. This is probably the most important group of flavor chemicals in red wines, but polyphenols are of much less importance in whites.

So what is phenol? It's a chemical that consists of a benzene ring, or C_6H_6 (six carbon atoms joined in a ring, with a hydrogen atom attached to each), with a hydroxyl group (-OH) substituted for one of the hydrogens: C_6H_5OH. Phenol is an important industrial chemical, but we're interested here in phenolics that are naturally synthesized by plants, built up of one or more phenol groups, modified in various ways, and joined together. There are more than eight thousand different phenolic compounds produced in plants.

An important property of phenolic compounds is that they associate spontaneously with a wide range of other chemical entities, such as proteins and other phenolic compounds, by means of non-covalent forces. A covalent bond is what we usually think of when we talk about chemical reactions, when two atoms combine by sharing electrons. A non-covalent bond is weaker and doesn't involve sharing electrons, but it's a common way of joining macromolecules together, for example through hydrogen bonding and hydrophobic (water-repelling) effects.

So let's look at some of the phenolic compounds that are important in wine. Alas, more chemical names are inevitable here. First, though, we need to consider the structure of the grape berry, because different bits contain different compounds. So let's go from the outside in. The skin has two types of cells, an outer layer of clear epidermal cells and then several layers (around six, but it depends on the variety) of hypodermal cells. Then there are three different pulp tissues: the outer and inner mesocarp and the vascular tissue that separates them. Then we have the seed, which has two layers of seed-coat (testa) cells— the outer layer, or cuticle, and the lignified inner testa cells— separated by a layer of thin-walled parenchyma cells that contains almost all of the seed phenolics. (Interestingly, seed browning is now thought to be caused by oxidizing of the tannins present in this layer, and not associated with the process of lignification.)

NON-FLAVONOID POLYPHENOLS:

THE PULP PHENOLICS

We'll begin in the pulp of the grape, with some polyphenols that are found in both red and white grapes. The first distinction to make is between flavonoid and non-flavonoid polyphenols, and we're starting with the latter. Generally speaking, these are found at low concentrations in grapes and wines, with one exception: hydroxycinnamic acids are the major phenolics in white wine (they are also found in red wine). Another group of non-flavonoid phenolics is the benzoic acids, such as gallic acid. The cinnamic and benzoic acids are small molecules that are often present in grapes in a conjugated form (e.g., as esters or glycosides). These are easily extracted from the pulp of grapes during pressing and occur at levels of 50–250 mg/L. Typical levels in finished wines would be around 130 mg/L.

Other non-flavonoid phenolics found in wine include the hydrolyzable tannins (such as gallic and egallic acids), which come from oak barrels; the volatile phenols (such as 4-ethylphenol, produced by *Brettanomyces*); and stilbenes (important in plant disease resistance, including celebrity stilbene, the phytoalexin resveratrol).

FLAVONOID COMPOUNDS: THE SKIN AND SEED PHENOLICS

These are the major phenolic compounds in grapes, and most of them are found in grape skins, but they also come from seeds and stems. This is where we bump into the two most famous types of polyphenols—anthocyanins and tannins. The flavonoid phenolics are categorized into two groups: flavan-3-ols and flavonols.

FLAVAN-3-OLS First, we have flavan-3-ol monomers. These are responsible for bitterness in wine, and they may also have an astringent taste. The major ones are (+)-catechin, (−)-epicatechin, and (−)-epicatechin-3-*O*-gallate. These are formed before veraison and change with ripening. They mostly come from seeds.

Then we have polymers of flavan-3-ol subunits, which are generally referred to as *condensed tannins* or *proanthocyanidins* (or *procyanidins*). These are responsible for astringency in red wines and come from the hypodermal layers of the skin and also the parenchymal layer in the seed coat.

Most of the subunits that make up tannins are either catechin or epicatechin, and these can be modified in various ways. The length of this chain—the polymer length—can vary from two or three subunits to over thirty. The length of the chain is called the *degree of polymerization* (DP), so a 10 DP chain of tannins has ten flavan-3-ol subunits in it.

Skin tannins are usually much bigger than seed tannins, and they may contain some epigallocatechin subunits. Seed tannins are smaller and lack epigallocatechin subunits. They also have a higher proportion of epicatechin gallate, which is rarely found in the skin tannins. In the grape skins, tannins will have a DP of up to 20. In seeds, the average DP is 15.

Tannins in berries change during the ripening process. In the skin, there's little change in the quantity of tannin from veraison to harvest, but the DP changes significantly. From green to red berries the average increases from 7 to 11, and at harvest DP is around 30.

One of the reasons why tannins are important in wine is the way they affect its mouthfeel. We sense tannins by a mixture of taste and touch. Tannins can have a bitter taste, especially when they are smaller (with a low DP). But the main way we sense them is by touch: they are astringent. They bind to proteins in our saliva and then the tannin–protein complexes precipitate, giving a drying sensation in the mouth.

It's interesting to think about why tannins might be doing this in our mouths. Plants form tannins as defense molecules, both to defend against microbial attack and, because plants are extremely vulnerable to being eaten, to act as antifeedants (chemicals that cause a pest, such as an insect, to stop eating). Plants are literally rooted in place, and so they have had to go to great lengths to make themselves unpalatable, acting as chemical factories to produce a wide range of toxic defensive secondary metabolites, as well as developing physical defenses such as thorns and stings.

One of the key roles of salivary proteins is to protect us from the harmful effects of tannins by binding to them and precipitating them before they reach the gut. This makes the plants more edible than they otherwise would be, neutralizing one of their defenses. If the salivary proteins didn't cause this precipitation, the tannins would interact with digestive enzymes (which are also proteins) in our gut and render them ineffective. This would reduce the palatability of plant components by making them much less digestible. The aversive taste of unripe fruits is due, in part, to high tannin concentrations. Along with color changes and high acid/low sugar, this is a way for the plant to prevent the fruit from being consumed before the seeds are ready for dispersal. We find the bitter taste and astringent sensation of tannin aversive and, as with such unpleasant oral sensations, the aversion can protect us from harmful consumption. Thus, the salivary proteins are potentially filling two roles. They allow us to detect tannins in food and to reject the food if the concentrations might be dangerous, while also helping neutralize any tannins present in food that is to be ingested.

One of the protein types found in our saliva is mucin, which is involved in forming a lubricated, slippery protective layer over the internal surface of the mouth. Tannins remove this lubrication, causing a sense of dryness and puckering. This is what we describe as "astringent." If you are unfamiliar with this sensation, you should try tasting a firm, unripe Hachiya persimmon.

Related to astringency is the taste of bitterness. The majority of tannins are chiefly sensed as astringent, but they can also be tasted as "bitter" when they are small enough to interact with bitter receptors on the tongue. Tannins seem to reach their most bitter taste at a DP of 4; they then decrease in bitterness and increase in astringency, which peaks at a DP of 7 (according to some studies, at least—others suggest it carries on increasing to 20 DP), before becoming steadily less astringent as they become larger. The astringent nature of tannins can be moderated by the presence of polysaccharides (sugars) or other wine components. It is also modified by the chemical adornments that tannins can grab, and there are many of those. In wine, tannins are continually changing their length (i.e., DP) and adding things to their structure. So, structurally, wine tannins can be incredibly complicated, and researchers are still trying to correlate mouthfeel properties with structure.

Interestingly, tannins are more astringent with lower pH (that is, wines with higher acidity taste more astringent, even with the same tannin content) and less astringent with increasing alcohol. However, the bitterness of tannins rises with alcohol level and is unchanged by pH changes.

Fining—the addition of proteins such as egg white or gelatin to a wine—doesn't actually remove much tannin. The popular idea is that the proteins bind to tannins, which then precipitate out. What happens is that the proteins do bind to tannins but largely remain in the wine, forming colloidal or soluble complexes that likely have reduced astringency.

ANTHOCYANINS Anthocyanins are the main pigments in wine, responsible for the color of red wines. They are found along with tannins in the hypodermal cells of the skin, except in *teinturier* (red-fleshed) grape varieties, where they are also found in the pulp. Fei He and colleagues have published a detailed review on anthocyanins for anyone wanting to dig deeper.[2]

Over six hundred anthocyanins have been identified in nature, and these are formed from six basic anthocyanidin structures, called *aglycones*. These are cyanidin (Cy), pelargonidin (Pg), delphinidin (Dp), petunidin (Pt), malvidin (Mv), and peonidin (Pn). They differ slightly in color, some being more red and others more purple. Anthocyanins are the combination of an anthocyanidin connected to a sugar (glycone) molecule, making the proper name for one grape anthocyanin *malvidin-3-glucoside*. Anthocyanins also differ in color according to pH, with a more red color at low pH and a more blue color at high pH. This can be seen when you use tap water to rinse out a wine glass with a tiny bit of red wine in it: the rise in pH causes the trace of wine to go from red to blue-black.

These basic aglycones are not very stable but may be modified by chemical processes called *glycosylation* and *acylation,* which improve their stability. The acylation can take place with the addition of acetic, *p*-coumaric, and caffeic acids. With these sorts of modifications, there can be up to twenty different anthocyanins in red grapes, depending on the variety. It's interesting to note that Pinot Noir lacks acylated anthocyanins, which explains why Pinots are usually paler in color than most other red wines, and in contrast Cabernet Sauvignon contains an almost full suite of eighteen of the twenty anthocyanins. Indeed, the anthocyanin profile can be used as a fingerprint of the grape variety, but this is useful only with fresh grapes: by the time a wine has been made, the anthocyanins will have been modified enough for this no longer to work.

The anthocyanins can exist in several equilibrium forms in wine. One of these is the flavylium ion, a very important form because it is red. Another form is the quinoidal base, which is blue. Only a small proportion of anthocyanins are in these colored forms in wine. It follows that if more of the anthocyanins are in the flavylium or quinoidal form, the wine will have more color. When sulfur dioxide is added to wine, it has a bleaching effect because it binds some of the anthocyanin as a colorless bisulfate adduct.

On their own, anthocyanins are unstable in wine—and, while they are responsible for color in grapes and juice, surprisingly they aren't that important for the long-term color of red wines. What else is involved in coloring the wine, then? Well, in addition to the anthocyanins, there are two major fermentation- and aging-derived color groups. The first of these is the pigmented polymers, formed by the chemical linkage between tannins and anthocyanins. This is a covalent (strong) linkage and is very important in forming stable color in wines. The evidence suggests that most of the pigmented polymer formation occurs during fermentation; but according to some reports, by the end of fermentation about 25 percent of the anthocyanins are thought to be complexed with tannins, and in barrel-aged reds this figure can rise to 40 percent within a year. Barrels help because they provide a bit of exposure to oxygen, which helps in forming these complexes, as well as supplying some extra tannins. Acetaldehyde, the product of the oxidation of alcohol, helps form these bonds. During fermentation, the formation of tannin–anthocyanin complexes helps retain more of both tannins and anthocyanins in the wine, as it makes them more soluble and stops them from dropping out as a deposit. These polymeric pigments also help with color intensity: around two-thirds of the anthocyanins are in a colored form when they are complexed with tannins, as opposed to around 10 percent of the free anthocyanins that are in a colored form.

Then there's another group, the anthocyanin-derived pigments, which arise from reactions between anthocyanins and other phenolics and aldehydes. Called the *pyroanthocyanins,* this large, complicated class of pigments is an area of intense current research, with new members being added all the time. The pyroanthocyanins—including the vitisins, portisins, and oxovitisins—are stable and resistant to sulfur dioxide bleaching. Most of them have a yellow-orange color, with the exception of portisins, which are blue.

The phenomenon of copigmentation needs a mention.[3] The colored anthocyanins (red flavylium or blue quinoidal base) are planar structures, and these can react with other planar structures (copigments) such that they form a molecular stack that excludes water. This protects the anthocyanins from hydration, increases the color intensity, and shifts the color towards purple. The copigments are usually other phenolic compounds, and in particular the flavonols, which we will discuss below. This is one of the reasons that red grapes are sometimes co-fermented with a small proportion of white grapes: the white grape skins provide copigments, so although you'd expect that the white grapes would reduce the color of the wine, they don't. In fact, the opposite occurs. The classic combination is a small proportion of Viognier together with Syrah/Shiraz. But flavonol concentration is also increased by exposure to ultraviolet (UV) light, so you might expect grapes that have experienced higher sunlight exposure to show a deeper color through increased copigmentation effects. However, in an aged red wine, the copigmentation effect is lost because the anthocyanins have been converted to wine pigments.

FLAVONOLS   The final group of phenolic compounds we will look at is the flavonols. They are found in the skins of both red and white grapes and act as sunscreens against UV-A and UV-B light wavelengths. Flavonol levels increase in response to enhanced UV exposure. They have a yellow color, which can contribute to the color of white wines but which is masked in red wines. The most important of the flavonols is quercitin, but kaempferol, myricetin, laricitrin, isorhamnetin, and syringetin are also found. White grapes lack myricetin, laricitrin, and syringetin.[4] Flavonols have high antioxidant capability, but perhaps their most important role is as copigments with anthocyanins to increase the color of new red wines.

The Role of Phenolics

These phenolic compounds have an important role to play in oxidation.[5] As noted earlier, wine wouldn't oxidize without copper and iron. It also wouldn't oxidize without phenolic compounds. Specifically, we are interested here in phenolics that include a particular chemical structure, namely *o*-diphenols (catechol and most other wine phenolics have this feature). These include gallic acid, caffeic acid, caftaric acid, epicatechin, catechin, and all flavan-3-ols. Remember the distinction between pulp phenolics and skin/seed phenolics? The hydroxycinnamate acids are the most common of the pulp phenolics, and so these are frequently the most commonly found phenolics in white wine. Caftaric acid, the most widely found hydroxycinnamate found in grapes, consists of caffeic acid bound to tartaric acid, and in wine this is hydrolyzed by yeasts during fermentation to form caffeic acid, which then becomes the most common hydroxycinnamate acid in wine. Catechin and epicatechin are the basic units of grape and wine tannins found in the skins and stems. If you press more heavily, and/or if there's more contact between juice and skin, you get more catechin and epicatechin in the wine. Their concentration correlates with browning susceptibility in white wine. Most of the literature suggests that the skin/stem phenolics are responsible for the browning potential of white wines, while some studies suggest that the level of *o*-diphenols (including pulp and skin/stem phenolics) in white wines is correlated to their ability to brown. Overall, the evidence seems to point to the skin/stem phenolics as most responsible.

Returning to the oxidation story we began earlier, the *o*-diphenols are very reactive with the hydroperoxyl radical, which is created when iron reduces oxygen. In this process, the diphenol is oxidized to a semiquinone, and then to a quinone. Some chemists theorize that this happens without the formation of the radical, but the outcome is the same. These quinones are reactive, and they will go on to react with wine components such as thiols or other phenolics. Hydrogen peroxide is also produced in the same process that produces quinones. Hydrogen peroxide is itself relatively unreactive, but if iron is present, it reacts with it to form the hydroxyl radical (OH; this process is called the *Fenton reaction*), which will then react with any molecules present in the wine, in proportion to the amount of those molecules present. Thus, the hydroxyl radical reacts with ethanol, which is relatively abundant, and the result is acetaldehyde. And organic acids will be oxidized to keto acids. This point is one that has become a little controversial of late. Some wine scientists, notably Roger Boulton of the University of California, Davis, suggest that the Fenton reaction doesn't occur in wine. "It can't occur in wine," says Boulton. "If you read Fenton's paper, first it depends on light. So the oxidation in a tank or a barrel isn't related to Fenton. [Secondly,] we don't get the reaction products that Fenton would give us." He explains: "Fenton's reaction was with tartaric acid in the presence of Fe(II) and the end product is glyoxylic acid. You don't get glyoxylic acid in wine. If you put light into a wine and give it air, you get glyoxylic acid. If you take the light away you won't."

Glutathione is interesting and needs a bit of further investigation. It can limit the oxidation of phenols by reacting with caftaric acid, generating 2-S-glutathionyl caftaric acid, also known as "grape reaction product" or GRP. If sufficient levels are present in wine after fermentation and in bottle, it can protect thiols (important sulfur-containing odor compounds in wine) from being oxidized by competing for the quinones, as well as helping preserve other aroma compounds such as iso-amyl acetate, ethyl hexanoate, and linalool. Glutathione also helps prevent the development of sotolon, one of the compounds associated with oxidized characters in white wines. So more glutathione is usually a good thing for white wines.

In summary, phenolics contribute to oxidation. Paradoxically, though, they also have a protective role against oxidation in red wines and skin-contact whites. This is because in those wines, there are enough polyphenols present that they can effectively put out the fire that the combination of oxygen, phenolics, and metal ions started in the first place. For this reason, red wines are able to absorb quite a bit more oxygen than whites without dele-terious effects.

SULFUR DIOXIDE AND OTHER ANTIOXIDANTS

So let's look at the role of sulfur dioxide (SO_2) and other antioxi-dants in wine. Sulfur dioxide is pretty much universally added to wine, both as an antimicrobial and also to protect against the damaging effects of oxygen. It reacts with the two key interme-diates of oxidation, the quinones and hydrogen peroxide, thus preventing—or, more precisely, reversing—oxidation. Sulfur dioxide doesn't really react directly with oxygen.

For every 1 mg of oxygen consumed, you'd expect 4 mg of free SO_2 to be consumed if SO_2 is doing its job in protecting the wine. If this ratio is below 4, then other oxidation reactions are occur-ring besides the consumption of SO_2. In experiments looking at this, Andrew Waterhouse and colleagues found a wine where the ratio was 1, suggesting that SO_2 was doing a poor job here. Indeed, the sensory work reported that this wine tasted oxidized. (Interestingly, the SO_2 worked better in wines that had been aged on lees, and the ratio in those wines was higher.) The researchers noticed that the wine had relatively little pyruvic acid. Although pyruvic acid doesn't bind to SO_2 as strongly as aldehyde does, it binds strongly enough that it creates bound SO_2 that is unable to react to protect the wine. Thus, they point out, pyruvic acid and other substances can bind SO_2 so that it is no longer available as a protective material, but when people do titrations for free SO_2 the latter has been released from these weak binders, such that the level of free SO_2 is overestimated. This could be an explanation for the common observation that white wines begin to show signs of oxidation when their free SO_2 level drops below 10 mg/L. When wines are barrel aged on lees, the yeasts and bacteria are able to break down any ketones and aldehydes present, reducing them to the alcohol form. So the wine contains fewer of the weak binders, and the wine will therefore be better protected at the same level of free SO_2.

Ascorbic acid (vitamin C), one of the most famous of all antioxidants, is used in wine. The concept is straightforward: by adding an extra antioxidant in addition to SO_2, the wine is protected more than it would be with SO_2 alone—a sort of belt-and-braces approach. And this might permit the use of lower SO_2 levels. But in practice it is more complicated. It seems that ascorbic acid may have a pro-oxidative role, depending on the levels of both these compounds in the wine. If ascorbic acid is used in combination with SO_2 at relatively low levels, it can accelerate both consumption of SO_2 and browning reactions, so it should be used with extreme caution, and always with plenty of SO_2.

INTERVIEW WITH MAURIZIO UGLIANO

I caught up with Dr. Maurizio Ugliano, a wine scientist previously with the AWRI and at that stage working for closure company Nomacorc, to ask him to help explain just what is going on in wine oxidation. It's useful to read his answers, which recap many of the complicated ideas that we have already discussed.

What happens when oxygen comes into contact with wine? It isn't straightforward, is it?

MAURIZIO UGLIANO: No. If we take the aroma compounds that we have in the wine and we put them in contact with oxygen in water, most of them will just stay as they are. What happens is that the oxygen interacts with a lot of things that have nothing to do with the aroma fraction, particularly phenolics, and through that first interaction you will generate species that will then drive a lot of chemical reactions in wine. You have a first interaction between oxygen and phenolics, and the outcome of this reaction will be the reactive species that will then be able to affect aroma precursors and aroma compounds, and push the wine towards oxidation.

What about metal ions? We heard someone say that in the absence of the transition metal ions, there wouldn't be any oxidation at all.

MU: You need metal ions to start the reaction between phenolics and oxygen. In the absence of metal ions such as iron or copper, this would not happen. What we have observed when we have tried to see whether the concentration of metals was one of the drivers for oxidation, was that the concentrations of metals that we have today in the wine industry are not making any difference. If we add metals to different levels, staying in the range that is reported from studies, we don't observe a difference in oxidation.

So the metal ions are necessary but they are not the limiting factor in oxidation?

MU: Not at the concentrations that we see today. When we measure metals in the wine, we measure by atomic spectroscropy, so we measure total metals. The metals could be bound or chelated to many different things. So the fact that the wine has a very high content of total metals, such as iron, doesn't mean that the iron is available for oxidative reactions. There could be wines that have a lot of iron, but which don't oxidize because the iron is bound to something else. It is a little bit of an approximation when I say that we look at metal levels in wine. It is not so easy to extract the information about how much iron is actually available. So far we can't really say that metals would make a difference.

So are phenolic compounds necessary to generate reactive oxygen species that then go and do the damage?

MU: Yes, phenolics are important.

In white wines as well?

MU: In white wines in particular, but in both. There have been a lot of studies done recently in France, and we did one in Chile looking at catechin and epicatechin, the so-called flavonoids. They interact with oxidation through this mechanism that involves iron and copper, and they form quinones. Quinones are very powerful reactive agents: for example, they can react with amino acids and form aldehydes. Today, a lot of what we observe as oxidation, especially in white wines, is not the contribution of aldehydes, but the loss of the fruity aromas that are due to thiols. In Sauvignon Blanc, oxygen plays a big role in the natural decay of the passionfruit fruity aromas. We think that a lot of the oxidation concerns that exist in the wine industry today should be more directed to managing this loss of fruitiness, rather than simply looking at oxidative faults. Wines end up flat and not expressing the characters that you'd expect.

What happens when there is sulfur dioxide in the wine? Is the oxygen first of all reacting with the sulfur dioxide?

MU: No. Sulfur dioxide will be recycling the quinones back to the original, nonreactive phenolics. But they will consume sulfur dioxide, which will also bind directly to these reactive species, blocking them in a state where they will not be reactive any more. Sulfur dioxide doesn't really react with oxygen. It is a very slow rate of reaction.

So when sulfur dioxide is binding up the products of the initial oxidation step, does it capture all of them, or do some get away and cause a little bit of oxidation—some collateral damage?

MU: It is difficult to answer the question because there haven't been many studies on this. A lot has to do with how much is around. If you have enough sulfur dioxide, you can in theory catch all the reactive species, but this would be a transient scenario because in this reaction sulfur dioxide will be consumed. Relatively quickly you would get to the point where there is not enough anymore. So there are going to be some that escape the blocking capacity of sulfur dioxide and just do other things. The interesting part is that some of the other things that these reactive oxygen species can do is react with other phenolics. So the phenolic component itself has a buffering capacity in the wine to prevent the onset of the negative oxidative mechanism, which could be aroma oxidation. There is also the role of other phenolic parts in blocking these reactive phenolics. We don't understand this very well yet, because characterizing the phenolic fraction of a wine is not so simple. So we are not really capable of saying that a wine that has this particular family of phenolics in very high concentrations will be capable of blocking the presence of the reactive oxidative phenolics.

Is the redox potential interesting for wine?

MU: In itself as a measure, I don't think it is very interesting. It expresses such a transient state that it doesn't really mean very much. What is more interesting is that there are different ways of adding fingerprinting technique, looking at the fingerprint of a wine through analytical techniques. We hope in the near future that this will allow us to characterize the phenolic fraction in such a way that we'll be able to say a wine with this sort of fingerprint is more prone to oxidation, and so it might need more sulfite or other preventive measures. There are many recent studies done with mass spectroscopy, in which a very simple analysis is done requiring no sample preparation. This can allow you to semi-quantify two hundred to three hundred nonvolatile compounds. In

New Zealand a guy has been working on cyclic voltammetry, which could be a way to fingerprint the phenolic composition of a wine. It is not so easy, though. We look at oxidation from the point of phenolics or sulfur dioxide. There is also the fact that if we look at aroma oxidation, in particular at aldehyde formation, you will need a precursor to form aldehyde. It could well be that the wines that are more prone to exhibit oxidation, everything else being the same, are the ones that have more precursor.

Is the alcohol itself oxidized?

MU: Yes, the alcohol will be oxidized to acetaldehyde. More typically, when we observe aroma oxidation at an early stage, there is not very much acetaldehyde. It is not very powerful as an aroma compound. Whereas you have other aldehydes like methional or phenylacetaldehyde that are a lot more powerful. They will be in the range of micrograms per liter.

Could the amino acid composition be quite important in the wine?

MU: It could be. This is what people are starting to take into consideration. This links back into a lot of other things that people may not consider when we talk about fermentation. Amino acids are in the grapes and are also altered during the fermentation process, because yeasts and bacteria will take a lot of these acids for their own metabolism. It could well be that at some point we start realizing that some wines that oxidize easily are those that contain some precursors that have been generated during fermentation, or have been left behind (not used)

by fermentation. There was a study done in Bordeaux
some years ago where they looked at an aroma compound
called *sotolon,* which is one of the oxidation markers. They
asked where this came from. They found out that among
other things it comes from a keto acid that is produced by
the yeast. There are yeasts that produce more of these
and yeasts that produce less.

*Glutathione is interesting, because it seems that some of the results are
counterintuitive. You can buy inactivated yeast products that give
a legal way of adding glutathione to the wine, and you'd assume
that glutathione is going to protect the wine against oxidation. But
it seems that it is maybe not as simple as that.*

MU: There are different things to consider. In theory, yes.
We have observed that if you add pure glutathione to a
wine, you would protect it from oxidation. This is
because glutathione will protect those quinones. It is a
sulfur compond. If you put in the picture 3-mercaptohex-
anol (3-MH, a thiol important in wine aroma) and
glutathione, they both target the quinone. Glutathione
will compete with 3-MH and consume part of the
quinone in a way that has no sensory implication. This is
the concept. But not all of these preparations are the
same. When we add glutathione alone it is quite unstable
and goes away pretty quickly, so fairly heavy doses are
needed to see any effect. In these preparations, there
could be other thiol compounds: there might be D-pep-
tides and cysteine. They all act in this competitive way to
block quinones and other oxidative species. In our
experience, glutathione in these types of preparations can
make life complicated from the winemaker's point of view

because you have another family of sulfur compounds which are the bad guys, responsible for reduction. They will be part of this same competitive scheme of reactions. You have hydrogen sulfide, 3-MH, glutathione. If glutathione is blocking the quinones you will preserve 3-MH as much as hydrogen sulfide as much as methylmercaptan. So you are creating a protective environment for all aroma active sulfur compounds. Glutathione doesn't have a sensory role, but the implication of having it in the wine will act at the level of all the other sulfur compounds.

QUALITY LOSS THROUGH OXYGEN MISMANAGEMENT

We have discussed oxygen with respect to the specific fault of oxidation. There's another important discussion we need to have, and this concerns the loss of quality through poor oxygen management, as mentioned briefly by Maurizio Ugliano above. There are several stages in winemaking where wines see oxygen. During fermentation—and particularly with red wines—this is something that is quite positive, because it helps the yeast do their job. Oxygen during fermentation strengthens the cell walls by encouraging sterol synthesis, and yeasts are then better able to resist the stresses that come later as the alcohol levels rise. This also applies to white-wine ferments—aerating an active ferment doesn't lead to oxidation, because the oxygen is scavenged by the yeasts—but fewer winemakers actively aerate their white-wine ferments. Oxygen at this stage helps encourage the formation of stable color in red wines, and the transformations, such as the development of tannin–anthocyanin complexes, help modify the mouthfeel of red wines also. After this, the contribution of limited oxygen exposure can be positive or negative, depending on the wine style.

Using relatively inexpensive oxygen-monitoring devices, it is possible for wineries to carry out thorough oxygen audits, and this is needed: very few wineries have any idea how much oxygen they are introducing into their wine through different stages of the winemaking process. The noise in the system from poor oxygen management obliterates the nuances of wine-style fine tuning that closures with a variable oxygen transmission rate (OTR) are capable of. Nomacorc's Dr. Stéphane Vidal explains the concept of oxygen management in wines as consisting of three phases. First, there is macro-oxygenation, which is the relatively large dose of oxygen that wine experiences during primary fermentation. Then there is micro-oxygenation, the smaller exposure to oxygen that occurs during barrel aging, or during aging in tank, with the deliberate introduction of small doses of oxygen. Finally, there is nano-oxygenation, which is the very limited exposure to oxygen that occurs after bottling through closure oxygen transmission. He points out that it makes little sense to suddenly alter this sequence by exposing wine at bottling to a high dose of oxygen (macro-oxygenation again), which is what commonly happens with poorly managed bottling conditions. It is worth emphasizing here that poor oxygen management at bottling is perhaps the biggest single factor in oxidative quality loss in bottled wine. A good bottling line should result in oxygen pickup of less than 1 mg/L. One concept that needs to be considered here is that of total package oxygen, or TPO. For bottling with a cork, this will consist of the oxygen dissolved in the wine, the oxygen in the headspace, and the oxygen dissolved in the closure itself, which will then find its way into the wine, over a period of around three months. In thinking about oxygen pickup and winery movements, temperature must also be considered. As with all gases, oxygen is much more soluble in cold wine. So racking a wine at low temperature increases the capacity of that wine to pick up oxygen during the process. Examples of oxygen pickup from winery operations:

- Careful pumping of wine from tank to tank with inert gas cover: o.i–o.2 mg/L
- Less careful pumping of wine from tank to tank without inert gas cover: up to 5 mg/L
- Centrifugation: 1.0 mg/L
- Protected pump-overs: 2.2 mg/L
- Aerative splashing pump-overs: 7.4 mg/L
- Bottling under ideal conditions: less than 1 mg/L

Results emerging from the Nomacorc-sponsored studies are beginning to fill in the significant gaps in our knowledge and bring this concept of winemaker intention closer to reality. In particular, there have been some interesting results coming from the laboratory of Dr. Véronique Cheynier at INRA Montpellier in France. Cheynier's lab has been studying the influence of oxygen on the evolution of polyphenolics in red wines made from Grenache. As discussed at length above, polyphenolic compounds are important in red wine and include the anthocyanins (which account for color) and tannins. To cut a very long story short, the anthocyanins and tannins change form throughout the winemaking process, combining with each other and other molecules. Exactly how they do this is very important for red-wine quality, and oxygen plays a major role.

For this research, Cheynier and colleagues created a matrix of sixteen different Grenache wines in order to compare extraction techniques, winemaking processes, and closure OTR. In the first instance, two extraction techniques were used: traditional maceration and flash release. Flash release (also known as *flash détente*) involves the rapid heating of grapes to 95°C for six minutes by steam and then cooling them down rapidly in a vacuum, thereby increasing the extraction of polyphenolic compounds from the skins. Then, after fermentation, each wine was further subdivided into two batches, one of which was subjected to microoxygenation whereas the other was not. These four different wines were then each bottled in 375 mL (half normal size) bottles in order to amplify the post-bottling effects of oxygen and were sealed with synthetic (Nomacorc) closures. Each of the four wines was subdivided further into four batches with varying OTR conditions, thus creating the matrix of sixteen experimental wines. The first batch was sealed with Nomacorc Light closures and stored in air (21 percent oxygen); the three remaining batches were sealed with Nomacorc Classic closures and stored in air (21 percent oxygen) or in stainless steel drums at 4 percent oxygen or 0 percent oxygen. All wines were kept at 23°C. Calculated OTRs for these four scenarios were 11.9, 8.0, 1.9, and 0.8 μg O_2 per bottle per day, respectively.

Using a technique called HPLC (high-performance liquid chromatography), the researchers were able to analyze the wines for a wide range of polyphenolic compounds. They also did analysis for free and total sulfur dioxide and looked at the color of the wines using spectrophotometry. The wines were studied ten months after bottling to look at the effect of post-bottling oxygen exposure. The researchers used principal component analysis (PCA) to compare the color and phenolic composition data from the sixteen different wines. PCA is a statistical technique used to find patterns in a mass of data. It pulls out from the data the factors that account for the variance in the variables under study—here the color of the wine and the phenolic composition. This showed that the most important factors in explaining the differences in these wines at ten months are (1) the OTR and (2) whether the wine was a flash release or a traditional maceration wine. Of twenty color and polyphenolic parameters measured, OTR had a significant effect on eighteen, extraction technique affected fourteen, and micro-oxygenation affected eleven.

The take-home message? After some time in bottle, closure OTR appears to have more influence on red-wine polyphenolics (and hence color, structure, and mouthfeel) than standard winemaking practices do. But this is just a chemical analysis, and what really matters is linking these changes detected by chemical analysis to changes in how the wines are perceived by consumers. Cheynier and colleagues therefore extended this study to sensory analysis.

In a second study, the same sixteen wines were subjected to sensory analysis by a panel of eighteen trained judges. The panel selected twelve attributes to describe these samples and then rated the wines blind for each, both at bottling (to assess the winemaking differences) and ten months after bottling. They found that OTR significantly affected eight of the twelve assessed attributes (while five attributes were affected significantly by winemaking at bottling, only one of these remained significant ten months after bottling). Wines stored under high OTR had more color intensity, appearing more orange, and had differences in odor (higher in "red fruits" and "caramel"; lower in "vegetable" and "animal"). These significant differences are interesting; even more interesting would be to present a range of wines, aged under a different OTR, to naive consumers to gauge their preferences.

Another interesting set of research results is coming from the AWRI's work on Sauvignon Blanc. Managing oxygen is particularly important for this variety, because it presents particular challenges owing to the fact that closely related volatile sulfur compounds can be both olfactory defects and desirable aromatics. There are three important sulfur-containing compounds that contribute to the aroma of Sauvignon Blanc: 3-mercaptohexan-1-ol (3-MH), 3-mercaptohexyl acetate (3-MHA), and 4-mercapto-4-methyl-2-pentanone (4-MMP), contributing aromas of grapefruit, boxwood, and passionfruit. These thiols (the name of the chemical class of these compounds) are susceptible to oxidation, and so the ideal closure for Sauvignon Blanc wines would seem to be the lowest-OTR closure possible, which is currently the screw cap with a tin–Saran liner. However, results from the AWRI's studies have also shown that using such a low-OTR closure can increase the risk of reductive aromas, owing to the shifts in sulfur compound chemistry that can occur in the low-redox-potential environment of a wine sealed this way. This creates a paradoxical situation, where winemakers who are using screw caps with tin–Saran liners play it safe by using pre-bottling copper fining to remove the sulfur compounds responsible for reductive off-flavors. The problem is that these sulfur compounds are very close in reactivity to the good thiols (3-MH, 3-MHA, and 4-MMP), which means that this copper fining can negatively affect varietal aroma.

The AWRI's research has shown that copper additions at bottling can reduce the concentration of 3-MH in Sauvignon Blanc wines. Interestingly, this effect was observed only at higher concentrations of SO_2 (60 mg/L) and not at lower concentrations (30 mg/L). But there was an even more interesting observation: after eight months of storage, even in the wines bottled with 30 mg/L of SO_2, a decrease in 3-MH, 3-MHA, and 4-MMP was seen in copper-fined wines that was larger, in most cases, than the decrease associated with the use of a higher-OTR closure. This indicates that for Sauvignon Blanc a winemaker is better off using a higher-OTR closure than using a tin–Saran screw cap in conjunction with copper fining. The authors point out that because copper is a powerful promoter of oxidation (a catalyst), excessive copper fining can accelerate oxidation reactions, resulting in a higher risk of premature oxidation.

WHAT ARE THE SENSORY CONSEQUENCES OF OXIDATION?

Oxidation causes a number of sensory changes to wine. But a distinction needs to be made here between oxidative characters in wine, which can be appropriate and positive for the wine style in question, and the term *oxidation,* which here implies a fault. We enter the territory of aesthetics here. How do we decide whether a wine is fine, but has some oxidative characters, or is merely oxidized? There are a number of famous wines that will split the room when tasters from different cultures are together, and here we have to rely on the community of judgment in appraising wines and making what is effectively a group decision on this point.

The first main chemical change is the oxidation of ethanol to acetaldehyde (also known as ethanal). This has an aroma of bruised apple and nuts, and it's usually the first clue that a wine may have seen too much oxygen. I often find in red wines that early signs of oxidation are a more open, fruity aroma coupled with the appley twist from acetaldehyde. Interestingly, Fino Sherry and Manzanilla both show quite a bit of acetaldehyde, but they are not oxidized; they need to be kept away from oxygen after opening and treated like normal white wines (keep in the fridge and drink within a few days) or they will deteriorate fast.

One of the main compounds associated with oxidation in white wines is sotolon (4,5-dinethyl-3-hydroxy-2(5)-furanone). At higher concentrations this has an intense curry aroma, and at lower levels it smells of walnuts, aged sake, and honey. It's also responsible for the dried-fig aroma found in Tawny Port and Vins Doux Naturels. Sotolon is seen as a universal marker for oxidation in white wines. Methional is another oxidation-related compound formed from the breakdown of methionine and smells of boiled potatoes and wilted roses. Phenacetaldehyde is yet another oxidation-related compound and has a distinctive note of honey. One compound found in red wines is MND (3-methyl-2,4-nonanedione), with aromas of hay, aniseed, and dried parsley, and this is associated with the pruney notes found in some prematurely aged red wines.

In addition to these aroma compounds, there are other sensory changes associated with oxidation and wine aging. The first is change in color. Whites get darker and become yellow/ gold/bronze/brown in succession. Reds lose their bright red/ purple hues and begin to develop brick red and brown notes. The bright fruity aromas typical of young wines fade and are replaced with more savory, earthy, nutty, and spicy notes. Sometimes this transition can be attractive, but when it occurs prematurely or in the wrong context it can be labeled oxidation. Often, these oxidative changes occur in parallel with the development of volatile acidity, the subject of the next chapter. It's the loss of positive, desirable characters in wine that's the major consequence of oxygen mismanagement in winemaking, and some wines that have lost quality in this way wouldn't be described as faulty but aren't as good as they could have been.

CHAPTER FIVE

Volatile Acidity

- **What is it?** The formation of acetic acid and related compounds by the action of bacteria during the winemaking process.

- **What is its flavor impact?** Acetic acid smells slightly vinegary, and ethyl acetate has a smell like nail polish remover.

- **What causes it?** Bacteria growing in the wine or on grapes and juice.

- **Is it always bad?** At low levels, volatile acidity can add a bit of a lift to the nose of wines and can be positive. But at higher levels it's objectionable.

- **How can it be prevented?** By avoiding oxygen contact during the winemaking process, good fruit selection, and creating an environment unsuitable for the bacteria.

- **How common is it?** Fairly common in barrel-aged reds and whites, and particularly in sweet wines.

Volatile acidity is, as the name suggests, that part of the acidity of a wine that is released as a vapor at room temperature and thus makes itself known on the nose—aromatic acidity, if you will. Winemakers normally split acidity measurements into three components, but there's some overlap between them. First is the total acidity, a measure of how much acidity is in the wine solution, and this is expressed as grams per liter, in terms of either tartaric acid equivalent or sulfuric acid equivalent (the latter measure is commonly used in France but not elsewhere). Then there is the measure called "pH": the lower the pH the more acid the solution (you'll probably remember this shown in school by litmus paper turning red), and the higher the pH the more alkaline it is (litmus paper turns blue). While pH is a really useful measurement for wine, it doesn't have an exact correspondence with the total acidity, for all sorts of complex reasons—and so both pH and total acidity are routinely measured. Finally, there is volatile acidity (VA), comprising mainly acetic acid but also lesser quantities of butyric, formic, and propionic acids. Another compound often talked about in the context of VA is ethyl acetate; this is produced by chemical modification (esterification) of acetic acid and has a smell of nail polish remover.

Just as all wines have acidity—it is a fundamental component—all wines have some VA. But although it is present in all wines, VA is something winemakers try to minimize, and it is almost always bad if it reaches a level where it can be detected, although at low levels it can add something to certain red wines. In this sense, it is one of those rarities: a wine fault that is a clear-cut problem, a fault to be avoided as much as possible. "Volatile acidity is always a problem," says wine consultant Pascal Chatonnet. "It's a fundamental problem of wine stability." Indeed, it's not possible to produce a wine without at least some VA, because acetic acid is produced in varying levels by all the microbes involved in fermentation, as well as being produced by acetic acid bacteria, which are present in all wines.

"Volatile acidity is produced by yeasts during fermentation," explains another leading winemaking consultant, Tony Jordan, "but most of the yeasts we use produce a level that is well below threshold." Under normal fermentation conditions, the classic wine yeast *Saccharomyces cerevisiae* produces up to 100 mg/L acetic acid. "There are some notorious VA-producing yeasts," adds Jordan, "so unless you want VA you avoid them. Wild yeast fermentations are more problematic. Often if they are slow to start or stick, volatile acidity becomes an issue." Under high-sugar conditions, *S. cerevisiae* can produce considerably higher levels of acetic acid; and lactic acid bacteria, which carry out malolactic fermentations in almost all reds and some whites, produce small amounts of acetic acid. But if alcoholic fermentation stops and the lactic acid bacteria start work on unfermented sugars in the must, the potential for acetic acid production is greatly increased. However, the chief microbes responsible for VA problems are the acetic acid bacteria.

There are two genera of acetic acid bacteria, *Acetobacter* and *Gluconobacter*. In wine and must, the most frequently encountered species are *G. oxydans, A. aceti*, and *A. pasteurianus*. These bacteria are quite common and are ideally adapted for growing in sugar- and alcohol-rich environments. Studies have shown that even under conditions where they aren't able to grow or proliferate, they persist in wine, ready to get going again should the wine environment suddenly become favorable for growth. The key fact about their biology worth noting is that their metabolism is aerobic: they need oxygen in order to grow. So, if at any stage in the wine's development the dissolved oxygen in it rises, the acetic acid bacteria will begin growing and producing acetic acid.

What do they do? In the presence of oxygen, *Acetobacter* oxidizes ethanol to acetaldehyde and then into acetic acid, while *Gluconobacter* prefers glucose, oxidizing it into ketonic compounds. As a result, *Acetobacter* is more common in wines where fermentation is underway and is the chief culprit underlying most VA problems, whereas *Gluconobacter* is more prevalent in musts and on grapes. *Acetobacter* can also turn the acetic acid it produces into ethyl acetate, which smells of nail polish and is detectable at about a quarter of the concentration of acetic acid.

The problem of VA can begin in the vineyard. All ripe grapes have populations of acetic acid bacteria on them—which is why all wines contain at least small populations of these bacteria—but rotten or damaged grapes have particularly high concentrations. In this case, because the grape skins are broken, fermentation can begin before the grapes are picked; in such conditions there is plenty of oxygen around, so the bacteria turn the alcohol into acetic acid, and as a result the must can already have a relatively high level of VA even before fermentation begins. It is estimated that for most wines, 50 percent of the final VA concentration is present at the start of fermentation. Wines made from botrytized grapes are typically higher in VA because the broken skins of these grapes harbor large populations of acetic acid bacteria. *Brettanomyces,* the rogue yeast that is one of the most commonly encountered problems in red-wine making, is thought to produce quite a bit of VA under aerobic conditions, but then it's likely that VA bacteria would also be present. This often contributes to the typical aroma of bretty wines, although it is hard to distinguish the contribution from each organism in this situation.

In the winery, the key to keeping VA levels down is good hygiene and protecting the developing wine from oxygen. Tony Jordan cites poor cellar hygiene, coupled with poor barrel topping or ullaged tanks without a good inert gas cover, as chief causes of VA in wine. Oxygen exposure is bad for two reasons. First, it reacts directly with components in the wine, modifying some of the important aroma components and also producing acetaldehyde, which makes the wine taste flat and oxidized. Second, there are viable populations of acetic acid bacteria in many wines, and given the right conditions these will grow. Their chief requirement is for oxygen, but they are also encouraged to proliferate by higher temperature and higher pH (less acid conditions). Each time the wine is exposed to another bit of oxygen, for example during racking, or if a barrel isn't topped up, they can grow a bit more and produce more acetic acid. Even when wines are protected by 25–30 mg/L of the universally used antimicrobial and antioxidant compound sulfur dioxide in its active free form—a very respectable level at normal wine pH that will keep a lid on microbial problems while it is maintained—the bacterial populations remain viable, waiting for their next chance to grow.

Topping up of barrels can make the problem worse, though, if it is performed too frequently. The act of taking the bung off and introducing fresh wine introduces oxygen, which encourages the growth of the bacteria. If a winemaker tops every week, the VA levels will just creep up. One solution is to top less frequently, but also to store the topping wine with very high levels of sulfur dioxide.

Climate change is also having an effect on VA in countries such as Australia, where heat waves during vintage are sometimes encountered. "In 2008 a winemaker said he could smell volatile acidity at crushing," says Adrian Coulter of the AWRI. "It was already taking off because of the bacteria even before fermentation. With the heat waves, there are compressed vintages. Everyone is trying to get their fruit off at once, but you can't get the harvesters. Bins are sitting out in the sun for ages. We see high volatile acidity and ethyl acetate."

If the winemaker has done their job properly, most finished wines will typically have acetic acid levels of 0.3–0.5 g/L (if yeasts typically make 100 μg/L, this means that the bacteria are contributing 200–400 μg/L). This is below the level at which we can detect it, or the "aroma threshold." The aroma threshold for acetic acid depends on the context of the wine and the sensitivity of the person sniffing, but it's between 0.6 and 0.9 g/L. Wine-producing countries have laws specifying the maximum allowable concentrations of acetic acid in wine. In the EU, for white and rose wines it is 1.07 g/L acetic acid, and for reds it is 1.2 g/L. In Australia it is 1.5 g/L, while the United States specifies 1.1 g/L for whites and 1.2 g/L for reds. There are usually special rules for wines that are barrel aged for a long time and for sweet wines, which may have more than this.

High levels of VA are also a problem because they can cause one of the winemaker's greatest nightmares: a stuck fermentation. Acetic acid bacteria produce yeast-inhibiting substances, and there is evidence that acetic acid itself is toxic to wine yeasts. Once a fermentation has "stuck"—in other words, the alcohol-producing yeast *S. cerevisiae* has stopped turning the sugar into alcohol, even though there is still sugar left in the must—the wine is at real risk: it's a sitting duck for the proliferation of even more acetic acid bacteria and the fermentation may never begin again.

What can winemakers do about VA? Their best bet is to prevent it from becoming a problem in the first place, and the most effective protective strategy is to keep air away from wine. I asked Tony Jordan whether he took steps to avoid VA in his winemaking. "All the time," he responded. "You need to be very careful with hygiene in equipment and storage vessels. You should make sure rigorous cellar practice is followed at all times, such as topping regimes, inert gas cover, and, of course, you should make sure you are tasting all your wines regularly and the lab is monitoring routinely for VA amongst other things."

In wines that are bottled young and kept during their development in stainless steel tanks, VA can fairly easily be avoided by not using damaged or rotten grapes, using sulfur dioxide sensibly, not letting the pH get too high, and using techniques such as blanketing the wine with inert gases. For wines that are aged for some time in barrel, this becomes a little more difficult; while similar strategies can be employed, one of the reasons for using barrels is to allow controlled exposure to oxygen during a wine's upbringing. In this case, it's especially important to keep the barrels topped up and to monitor the levels of free sulfur dioxide to ensure they are protecting the wine effectively against bacterial growth.

How can VA be spotted in a wine? Most well-made commercial wine styles don't show it. I have tasted wines spiked with both excessive acetic acid and excessive ethyl acetate. Acetic acid at 1.5 g/L adds a lifted, vinegary edge to the wine. Ethyl acetate, which is commonly found alongside acetic acid, adds a nail-polish-remover-like quality at 250 mg/L. At lower levels, VA can make itself known in more subtle ways. Australian wine judges have a descriptive term for the nose of a wine: *lifted*. A lifted nose is one where a little bit of VA is present, and it's sometimes found in red wines that have been barrel aged for a long time. It's not always a negative. Indeed, you could argue that a little bit of VA can be positive, something that Tony Jordan agrees with: "Volatile acidity just above threshold can look good in many reds. Apart from stickies, I don't like it in whites." He adds that VA "is very much part of many botrytis styles, though too much is too much." It is quite a challenge for winemakers to keep VA low in sweet wines, because the high sugar makes yeasts struggle a bit, and even more so in wines made from botrytized grapes because these will come into the winery with higher levels of acetic bacteria. "These are stressed fermentations," says Jordan, "but good attention to yeast selection, nutrient status throughout the ferment, and fermentation rate helps."

Another way to prevent excess VA is to use specific selected yeasts that are low producers. This can be particularly useful in white wines. The non-*Saccharomyces* yeast *Torulaspora delbrueckii*, which is now available commercially, is very useful for fermenting high-maturity grapes because it produces very low VA. For example, a Sauternes conventionally fermented might have 1.5 g/L volatile acidity, but with *Torulaspora* this can come down to 0.5 g/L. It is capable of fermenting to 10–11 percent alcohol, which is much more than most non-*Saccharomyces* yeasts, but the idea is to use it in combination with a selected strain of *S. cerevisiae* in a sequential inoculation.

Finally, what can winemakers do if they have a barrel or tank with a VA problem? There are three choices. The first is to dump the wine. The second is to blend it with a sufficient volume of wine with a low acetic acid level, so the final level of the wine is below aroma threshold. The third is to use reverse osmosis, a modern cross-flow filtration technique that strips out a colorless permeate consisting of water, alcohol, and small molecules, including the offending acetic acid. This permeate is then passed through an ion exchange column, which removes the acetic acid, and the remainder, now free of acetic acid, is recombined with the wine. Reverse osmosis and ion exchange can also be used on wines that have stuck in the middle of fermentation; once the acetic acid has been removed, fermentation often starts again.

CHAPTER SIX

Reduction and Volatile Sulfur Compounds

- **What is it?** *Reduction* is the common name for the above-threshold presence of volatile sulfur compounds (VSCs) in wine.

- **What is its flavor impact?** It varies. The most basic VSC is hydrogen sulfide, which smells of bad drains and rotten eggs. Other VSC aromas include cooked cabbage, onion, gunflint, and sweet corn.

- **What causes it?** It's caused largely by yeast metabolism. Yeasts produce these VSCs in certain conditions, such as low nitrogen availability. Some yeast strains produce more than others. Sometimes reduction develops after bottling, especially where low-oxygen-transmission closures are used.

- **Is it always bad?** No. Some of the VSCs can be positive, in the right wine context. In other cases, reduction is a nasty fault. In the case of polyfunctional thiols, they are a fundamental component of wine aroma in some varieties, such as Sauvignon Blanc. It all depends.

- **How can it be prevented?** By good fermentation management, appropriate racking, the right use of oxygen during winemaking, and correct bottling procedures.
- **How common is it?** It's relatively common, but it's quite rare to find really, really stinky reductive wines these days.

Reduction is one of the most complicated and intriguing of all wine faults. The term is used widely, but perhaps rather mis-leadingly, to refer to problems in wine caused by a family of VSCs. The origin of these compounds in wine is from a number of different sources, and the reason this is such an interesting group of compounds is that some can be the source of faults in some wines, but provide positive attributes in others. Indeed, VSCs are important in the aromas of many fermented foods and drinks, such as cheese and beer, but have the paradoxical ability to be both positive and negative, depending on the context and concentration. In particular, there are a group of VSCs known as *polyfunctional thiols* that are a vital part of varietal character in Sauvignon Blanc, and—as more research results become available—it turns out they are involved in wine aroma for many grape varieties. In this chapter, we are going to dig a bit deeper to get to grips with the various sulfur compounds involved and look at where they come from.

Why was the term *reduction* originally coined? These problems frequently occur in wines at a stage where they are protected from oxygen (such as aging on lees in barrels), and reduction, chemically speaking, is the opposite of oxidation. In any chemical reaction, electrons (which have a negative charge) are gained by one partner (that partner is reduced) while electrons are lost by the other partner (that partner is oxidized). Hydrogen sulfide (H_2S) is a reduced form of sulfur, as are the other VSCs that we are interested in when we discuss reduction. By contrast, SO_2, the almost universally used wine additive, is an oxidized form of sulfur.

Volatile sulfur compounds are known to be potent aroma compounds, with detection thresholds ranging from low ng/L to µg/L concentrations. This makes them a real problem for winemakers, because you don't need much of them to experience a significant sensory impact. Most are unpleasant-smelling, the notable exceptions being the long-chain polyfunctional thiols that contribute pleasant passionfruit, grapefruit, and tropical fruit aromas in white wines and enhance berry fruit characters in reds.

There is no single source of the VSCs that are found in wine and that contribute to reduction. The current picture is quite a complicated one, but one of the chief culprits is the process by which yeasts produce VSCs during fermentation. Currently, VSCs are believed to be produced by four mechanisms:[1]

1. Degradation of the sulfur-containing amino acids methionine and cysteine. Under laboratory conditions these have been seen to degrade, releasing H_2S. It's not totally clear that this occurs in fermentation conditions.

2. Reduction of elemental sulfur, which is widely used in vineyards as a fungicide. If elemental sulfur is present on grapes at harvest, it can be reduced by the reductive conditions of the fermentation process to generate H_2S, independently of yeasts. But this is not thought to be a big contributor, as long as the appropriate withholding

periods are respected and sulfur isn't sprayed close to harvest.

3. Direct reduction of sulfite or sulfate (this is thought to be quite rare).

4. The process that yeasts use to make sulfur-containing amino acids, during which sulfate is reduced. This process, the "sulfate reductase pathway," produces the majority of VSCs. When nitrogen in the must is limited, cysteine is accumulated by various permeases and degraded to H_2S, pyruvate, and ammonia by cysteine desulfhydrase. But there isn't enough cysteine present in grape must to account for the level of H_2S produced during fermentation by this pathway. However, cysteine can be made by yeasts from other sulfur-containing compounds, such as glutathione. If assimilable nitrogen (that is, nitrogen in a form that grapes can use it in) is limited in the must, there will not be enough O-acetyl-L-homocysteine present to catch all the H_2S that is formed.

Fermentation is a complicated process. One of the main reactions taking place is the action of yeasts to break down sugar, resulting in the production of alcohol. This provides energy for yeasts to grow. Moreover, a whole host of other chemical reactions will be taking place at the same time, including many complex interactions between the yeasts and compounds present in the grape must. Yeasts are also able to modify flavor compounds derived from oak barrels.

Most fermentations take place in the absence of oxygen, under anaerobic conditions. In addition to sugar, yeasts' nutrient requirements include nitrogen, phosphate, sulfate, potassium, magnesium, and trace elements. Vitamins such as biotin and pantothenic acid are also required. While oxygen isn't needed, if it is present it can help yeasts develop tolerance to alcohol by increasing the synthesis of sterols and unsaturated fatty acids that improve yeast membrane function. In fact, some yeast companies prepare yeasts in a high-oxygen environment before drying them, in order to make them more robust when they are used in fermentations.

It is important to realize that not all yeasts are the same. There are important strain differences, and in the case of wild fermentations there will be species differences. This makes it all very complicated indeed. The ways in which yeasts behave—and the sorts of flavor compounds they produce—result from a combination of yeast genetics and the environment, which includes the composition of the must, the temperature, and the presence or absence of oxygen.

Most musts are low in organic sulfur. *Organic* refers to chemical compounds containing carbon, and in this case we are referring to the amino acids that contain sulfur (cysteine and methionine) and glutathione. As a result, yeasts use the sulfate reductase pathway to produce organic sulfur compounds from sulfate and sulfite. This process starts with sulfate, which is converted to sulfite, which in turn is converted to H_2S. This H_2S is used as a building block for the various organic sulfur compounds. Sulfite also comes into the yeast cell from the sulfite added during winemaking, and if this is not pumped out of the yeast cell it can produce additional H_2S. If nitrogen supply to the yeast is limited, the next step in the sulfur pathway (which removes H_2S by forming sulfur-containing amino acids) can't happen, and H_2S builds up. This is then released by the yeast into the wine, resulting in off flavors.

Sulfate is accumulated by yeasts through two transporters

that are specific for sulfate. These are called Sul1p and Sul2p. It is reduced to H₂S by the "sulfate reductase assimilation pathway," the last step of which is conversion of sulfite to H₂S by sulfite reductase, an enzyme encoded by two genes, *MET5* and *MET10*. In addition, sulfite can enter yeast cells directly and then be directly reduced to H₂S. Cysteine and methionine are accumulated by specific permeases (Mup1p, Mup3p, Gap1p, and Yct1p). Low concentrations of these amino acids lead to the induction of the sulfate reductase assimilation pathway.

As an aside, yeast metabolism is one reason why wines fermented in wood are less oaky tasting than wines that are transferred to barrels after fermentation is complete. This is because yeasts are able to reduce vanillin to vanillic alcohol.

In the old days, copper fittings were common in wineries, and elemental sulfur was widely used in the vineyard. Perhaps people didn't realize that yeasts were important in producing VSCs. In old-fashioned wineries, I have seen copper plates on the edges of old barrels that the wine came into contact with when it was splash racked.

Fairly recently, both the AWRI and Linda Bisson at the University of California, Davis, have identified mutants of the pathway that are low-H₂S-producing strains. In fact, Bisson's strain is described as a zero-H₂S producer.[2] Bisson and colleagues found a strain of yeast that produced no H₂S because of a mutation in *MET10*, one of the genes encoding the sulfate reductase enzyme. Commercial strains of Bisson's low-H₂S producers have been released by the company Renaissance Yeast. The AWRI team also identified yeast strains with mutations in genes encoding sulfate reductase; in their case, H₂S production was reduced by 50–99 percent.[3] These strains have been made commercially available, but one drawback with them is that they can produce high levels of SO_2. Yeasts produce some SO_2 during fermentation, and this level can be quite high, depending on the strain. Normally it is below 10 μg/L, which is the level at which a wine is legally required to have "Contains Sulfites" on the label. But some strains exceed this, and a few by as much as a factor of ten. The low- or no-H_2S strains tend to produce more SO_2, and this can cause problems with malolactic fermentation, if this second fermentation is desired, because the lactic acid bacteria are quite sensitive to elevated levels of SO_2.

NUTRIENT SUPPLEMENTATION TO AVOID REDUCTION

The chief nutrient required by yeasts (and the one that's most often deficient in grape juice) is nitrogen, which is used for the production of amino acids (and thus proteins) by the yeasts. The nitrogen that's needed by yeasts is called yeast assimilable nitrogen (YAN) and consists of free amino nitrogen (FAN, which is made up of alpha amino acids and small peptides) and ammonium ions. A lack of sufficient YAN is a key risk factor for the development of reductive off-odors in wines. If there isn't enough YAN present, sulfide produced during the sulfate reductase pathway in yeasts builds up and is released from the yeast cells as H_2S.

Other microorganisms present in the must can also deplete nutrients. For example, during a pre-fermentation cold soak, other microbes can deplete nutrients before the yeasts get going; because sampling for YAN usually takes place at the juice stage, this change won't be picked up. There can be problems the other way, too: if you don't know the nutritional needs of the yeast strain you're using, you can supplement too much and leave nutrients in the wine to feed other microbes. Another risk of adding too much nitrogen is that it can result in flavor defects. Excess nitrogen leads to the production of acetate esters, especially ethyl acetate, which smells of nail polish remover. Typical YAN concentrations naturally occurring in must are 50–450 mg/L, the most common range being 100–200 mg/L. The recommendations are that, as a minimum, whites need 150 mg/L and reds 100 mg/L, with a more comfortable level being around 250 mg/L. The maximum demand from the yeasts is around 400 mg/L. As a rough guideline, 150 mg/L is the tipping point. Below this, it's likely you'll see some flavor impact from reduced nutrient availability, which causes reduction issues, and the risk of stuck ferment increases as well. Even when the ferment doesn't stick, slow, attenuated ferments can have a sensory impact on the wine that some people dislike, especially in varieties such as Pinot Gris, Riesling, and Sauvignon Blanc.

There are two different sorts of nutrients widely used in winemaking. The first, and least expensive, is diammonium phosphate (DAP), which is an inorganic nitrogen source. The second is a set of organic nitrogen supplements, most of which are based on yeast products such as inactivated dried yeast hulls. Yeast companies that supply cultured yeasts know their nutritional demands and can supplement what's necessary for reliable fermentations. They typically offer a range of products based on inactivated yeasts, and some are compatible with organics, too.

During their phase of active growth, yeasts need vitamins and minerals as well as nitrogen. Supplementing early with DAP can make it tricky for the yeast cells to absorb these from the must, so sometimes it is advisable to delay supplementation of the must. But later supplementation can promote the development of spoilage organisms and lead to biogenic amine production in the wine.

While DAP is the most popular nitrogen addition in winemaking, there's currently some discussion that this might be making the problems it's intended to solve worse. In terms of yeast performance, are there better things you can do? And is the amino acid content of juice important? "It is absolutely critical for all kinds of things," says Richard Gardner, a yeast researcher from the University of Auckland, New Zealand.

> But there is no cheap supply of amino acids available to add to grape juice. It is too expensive, so DAP is used. Lisa Van de Water [of Vinotec Napa, California] calls DAP "yeast candy." DAP changes the whole flow of metabolism in the cell. It changes amino acid pathways, which changes esters and changes thiols. I don't know how all of these things interact, and I suspect no one else knows. But if you give the yeast pure ammonium it changes the yeast cell in a major way. The best data come from the Australians: they say too little nitrogen and you are in fermentation trouble, and too much DAP and you get bad aromas. You need to be in the middle area. Too much DAP is bad; not enough nitrogen is worse.

Sam Harrop is a consulting winemaker who works widely in Europe and New Zealand. "I tend to supplement anything below 200 YAN," he says, "but I don't use DAP unless it's a commercial product where every cent counts." His preference is to use Fermaid O, which he adds twice: just after the start of fermentation and again a third of the way through. If he's making wine in a more mineral style, as with his own Cedalion Chardonnay from Waiheke Island, he'll intervene less and work with lower YAN levels. For a commercial Sauvignon Blanc, he might add a combination of DAP and Fermaid K for cost reasons. He thinks there's an increasing need to add nitrogen supplements because screw-cap closures are becoming more common, and most screw-cap liners have a very low level of oxygen transmission. "In aromatic styles, it's becoming more important to use nutrients to avoid the reductive characters and eliminate as many of the precursors as possible." He also thinks clean ferments are very important for rosé. "You really can't have any of those sulfides if you want the primary characters of the rosé [to stand out]."

REDUCTION AFTER FERMENTATION

Because it is quite volatile, H_2S can be lost from young wines during processes such as racking. But reduction problems often develop after fermentation has finished, when the wine is sitting in barrel or tank on yeast lees. There are two possible explanations for this. It could be that sulfide is arising from degradation of sulfur-containing compounds in the yeast lees. Alternatively, it could be that the sulfide produced by the yeasts during fermentation wasn't all released at the time, and some became chemically entrapped, bound to compounds or trapped in a non-volatile form in the wine. Then, during the changes associated with wine aging, this sulfide is released, creating a stinky wine.

TOYING WITH REDUCTION AS A COMPLEXING FACTOR IN WINE

Reduction is frequently a negative attribute in wine. No one likes their wines to smell of rotten eggs or drains. And the garlic, cooked-cabbage, or rubber aromas that can come from VSCs are rarely pleasant. But there are some VSCs that contribute positive aromas in wine. One of the most well-studied examples is that of the polyfunctional thiols that are an important part of varietal aroma in Sauvignon Blanc. Thiols, also known as *mercaptans,* are a subclass of VCSs with a sulfur atom bound to a hydrogen atom—the SH group (that is, the "sulfhydryl" or "thiol" group). There's a little confusion about naming, with two conventions in use. The first is to add the term *thiol* to the name of the other bit of the chemical structure; the second is to add *mercaptan.* So a compound with the formula CH_3SH can be called either *methanethiol* or *methylmercaptan,* though the former is preferable.

It's only relatively recently that the current picture of the importance of thiols in wine has emerged. In the 1990s, a collaborative research effort between Takatoshi Tominaga and Denis Dubourdieu (Université Victor Segalen Bordeaux 2) came up with surprising findings. They identified a number of thiols that are present in Sauvignon Blanc wines and that contribute, in part, to their distinctive varietal characteristics. It is these thiols, together with 2-methoxy-3-isobutylpyrazine (IBMP, usually referred to as "methoxypyrazine"), that are the "impact" compounds important in Sauvignon Blanc aroma. This pioneering work by the French group was hugely significant: it showed that as well as causing faults, volatile thiols add pleasant herbaceous, fruity, mineral, smoky, and toasty characters—not only to Sauvignon Blanc, but also to other white varieties such as Riesling, Muscat, Gewürztraminer, Colombard, Bacchus, Petit Manseng, and Chenin Blanc. Subsequent work has shown that they also contribute to the aromas of some red wines. This was a really interesting finding, and Tominaga, Dubourdieu, and colleagues went on to identify six volatile thiols in the Sauvignon Blanc wines they analyzed, of which three have proved to be most significant.

The most desirable is 3-mercaptohexyl acetate (3-MHA), which gives aromas of grapefruit zest and passionfruit. During aging of wine, 3-MHA hydrolyzes to the next most important,

3-mercaptohexan-1-ol (3-MH). This also smells of passionfruit and grapefruit, but it's a little less exotically aromatic. The third is 4-mercapto-4-methylpentan-2-one (4-MMP), which smells of box tree and broom. Sauvignon Blanc from New Zealand's Marlborough region is particularly high in 3-MH and 3-MHA. "I think there is a lot of thinking still to be done on reduction," says Maurizio Ugliano, whom we met in chapter 4.

To me what is important about reduction is that there are two families of sulfur compounds, and then there is this other family of two or three sulfur compounds in between which seem to be formed by the combination of the bad sulfur compounds with something else in the wine. You see the obviously good and the obviously bad sulfur compounds, but some of these obviously bad compounds will participate in forming some others that can be good.

He identifies a class of VSCs called *benzomercaptans* as being particularly interesting in this regard.

People are now beginning to understand, for example, how to make New Zealand–style Sauvignon Blanc with the fruity thiols, although no one seems to be capable of making it quite as intense as the New Zealand style, whereas the smoky, roasted, crème brûlée aromas typical of benzomercaptans are a bit more interesting. They could be much more an expression of different regions, or different winemaking styles.

He thinks that with more research and a better understanding of reduction, it could be managed in a way that allows winemakers to promote some of these interesting toasted, roasted aromas, without going too far into reduction.

There's more to good sulfur compounds than just the polyfunctional thiol characters of passionfruit and grapefruit. I guess this fits with the general knowledge that we've had for a long time, that in some cases reduction is part of the style of the wine. But we don't seem to be able to describe these cases very well, especially when we start talking about minerality and what it is. And from a chemical point of view, we don't seem to be able to understand which the compounds are that take the bad reduction into this complexity area. It is the complex sulfur aromas that we don't understand well, but it is an area where I think some interesting developments will follow.

He points out that individual differences and the context of the wine matter:

> In a tasting yesterday, when most people were saying that they really liked a wine because of the thiol passionfruit aromas, some people were saying they didn't like it because of sulfury aromas. People are variable in the way they perceive these aromas. When you get to the highest levels of fruity thiols in Sauvignon Blanc, for some it gets into the cat-urine state, and for some others it is just too strong and monodimensional: they can't smell anything else. So reduction is still a matter of debate.

The context of the wine can determine whether people find oxidation or reduction to be a problem.

> Some recent studies done by the aroma chemistry team at Zaragoza in Spain found that the highest-quality red wines they could analyze, in the 50 Euros and over range, had the highest concentration of reductive and oxidative aroma compounds. In this matrix, perhaps these compounds contribute to the complex nuances of these wines. Whereas probably if you imagine the same concentrations of these compounds in more simple wines, they would come out as dominant reduction or dominant oxidation. It is a lot to do with the matrix. This could affect the volatility. These aroma interactions are complex. We can take the same amount of a certain aroma compound and put it in the presence of other aroma compounds and we will smell it in a very different way.

Ugliano also highlights dimethyl sulfide (DMS) as a VSC that can be both positive and negative.

DMS is a classic example. We didn't think of DMS as anything important apart from the cooked asparagus/canned asparagus flavors you find in some wines that age for a long time. But it has been shown that a little bit of DMS promotes the expression of dark fruit/berry fruit character, even if the compound itself doesn't smell like that at all. It is quite an unpleasant-smelling compound, but it supports the expression of these fruity notes when it doesn't become dominant.... There are many examples like this, and we are missing an understanding of this from a practical point of view. I did a lot of work with fermentation and nutrients when I was in Australia. Other people always had a tendency to simplify these stories. For example, they'd say, these esters have been increasing with fermentation, and the threshold of these esters if we don't add nitrogen was below the threshold, and when we add nitrogen it is above threshold. The approach has been to isolate each compound from its context and talk about it individually, saying the effect of this variable is important on this compound because it is becoming above threshold and before it was below threshold. The reality is that when you have some manipulation that affects many things at the same time you can't study one compound in isolation and talk about an individual threshold. We currently don't look at these changes in a holistic matrix way. When we have a wine in a bottle with a high dose of oxygen, we are not forming reductive sulfur compounds, we are probably killing some of the existing compounds, including the good thiols, and we are forming some aldehydes and we might be forming some lactones, such as sotolon.

MATCHSTICK REDUCTION IN CHARDONNAY

Over the past five years or so, there has been growing interest in toying with reductive characters in white wines, particularly in

Chardonnay. It used to be a niche, insiders-only sort of topic, but of late it has been quite mainstream. New Zealand consultant winemaker Matt Thomson points out how many of the best domaines in Burgundy are masters at getting just the right level of struck-match mercaptan characters in their Chardonnays. He thinks that Michael Brajkovich of Kumeu River in New Zealand is also very good at this. Is this effect produced by yeasts? "I am not sure about the biochemistry of it, but we have found it comes early, so I don't think it's produced after fermentation," says Thomson.

> Once you get it, it seems to remain there. It seems stable with copper, too. I have also found it stable to ascorbic acid and copper. I have had it before in my wines and I think it's great.... Mike has told me how he gets it, through solids, and we have used solids. But what he told me is that instead of filling your barrels out of tank, when you get all the lees in the last couple of barrels and they stink like hell, he keeps the must homogeneous so there is a gentle mixing process going on while he fills the barrels. But there is more than this: I think the yeasts he has got resident in the winery are very good at producing this mercaptan. This is the other part of the story. This is why wild ferments work for some and not for others.

I asked him whether reduction can also work in reds as a complexing factor.

> Sometimes, but at a low level. Often, sulfides shut down the fruit, and this can be the problem. Often the wine can appear just slightly oxidized, with something shutting it down, and then you'll see some reduction. I have seen some struck-match notes in Pinot that I don't object to, and occasionally in Barolo, and also in cool climate Syrah. That bacon/juniper thing can work nicely with the struck-match note. I don't really like egg!

Michael Hill Smith, of Australian winery Shaw and Smith, says that the deliberate use of reduction is quite a new thing.

Particularly in Australia, anything that showed any reductive characters was always knocked. It was always seen as a wine fault and a bad thing. But then suddenly you get that wonderful edge of reduction character that is found in great white Burgundy, and you say, "How good is that?" You see it a lot now: winemakers are seeking gunflint, a little bit of funk, that is a wonderful thing as a complexing agent.

How does it happen? "At one stage our view was that it was at the back end—it came from leaving the wine on lees with zero sulfur at low temperature, stirring and building that character post-ferment," says Hill Smith. "But I am told that this is not the case: others tell me it us up front: it is to do with the beginning of fermentation. I love it in white Burgundy. It is not a fault that I am sensitive to. It doesn't bother me."

One popular method for getting nice reduction is known informally as the "Roulot method," after the famous white Burgundy producer. The technique here is to take the wine out of barrel and take it to stainless steel for the last six months of its *élevage,* where the reductive conditions tighten it up and add some matchstick minerality. Jean-Marc Roulot described his winemaking technique to me. Chardonnay grapes are hand harvested and whole-bunch pressed, but they are lightly crushed first, which is an unusual move. "We get most of the juice out at low pressure," he says, first of all pressing at 0.2 bar, then rising to 0.6. This gives 90 percent of the juice. He then goes up to 1.6 bar, but it's just for a small proportion of the juice. This allows him to have good pH and purity. "It contributes a lot to the style,'" he says. He then decants overnight, but he likes to keep a lot of the lees. After the decanting vat there is another vat, so that he can mix up the lees and have the same turbidity in each barrel. This takes place right above the cellar. "If a plot is harvested on Monday, by Tuesday morning it is in barrel," he says. The barrel room is very cool, and that's where fermentation takes place. Most of his barrels are of regular size, but he has three 1,200-liter Stockinger foudres, which he likes a lot. His favored cooper is Damy (based in Meursault). The proportion of new oak varies from 5 to 10 percent for the Bourgogne Blanc, to 15 percent for village, to a maximum of one-third for premier cru. The wines spend a full year in barrel with light battonage once every two to three weeks until the end of malolactic fermentation. The first racking is postponed as long as possible until the new vintage is near, so that the barrels are empty for only a short time. Then the wine is racked to stainless steel, taking the lees with it, for an extra six months. This is a vital step. "We get microoxygenation in the wood, then reduction in stainless steel," says Jean-Marc. "It gives the wine vertical tension. It is a shame so many people come to Burgundy in November to taste the vintage. The difference between then and January to March is huge."

"I really love that matchstick character," says Rick Kinzbrunner of celebrated Australian winery Giaconda, known for their complex Chardonnays. "More solids and the right type of barrel can increase the chance of getting it." Kinzbrunner says that he gets it only with new oak, which is something I haven't heard elsewhere. "The right type of barrels and toast can increase the chances. You can't get it in an old barrel. You get one barrel like that only in every forty barrels, and you only need half a dozen for it to carry through the whole wine. You don't want to overdo it." Rick had a special barrel designed with the most possibility of developing this matchstick character. It had a special char, and it was Vosges/Allier with special toast, three years air dried.

Kym Schroeter, white-wine maker at Australian winery Penfolds, has toyed with reduction but thinks that his 2009 Reserve

Bin Chardonnay borders on having too much of the matchstick character. "You have to be very careful about how much you add to your blend," he says. "You always get some sulfidic barrels, but you can go too far and get gas pipey and garlicky. I like to see a bit to add complexity, but I don't like to see it taking over a ferment."

POST-BOTTLING REDUCTION

With the widespread use of screw caps, some technical issues have emerged surrounding post-bottling sulfur chemistry, or reduction. It's has proved hard to discuss these issues dispassionately, because such is the volume of the war of words between advocates of the screw cap and of cork that these discussions rapidly get fanned into flames. Add to this that the subject matter itself is horridly technical, and the fact that we don't have all the data we'd like, and there's a need for calm, balanced treatment. But right at the start, it's important to get some perspective here. In Australia, screw caps have been used since 2000 and currently seal around 80 percent of bottles produced there. In New Zealand, they have been used since 2001 and seal around 95 percent of all Kiwi wine bottles. If there were huge technical issues with them, this level of adoption would never have happened. Much of the discussion that follows probably reflects teething problems that may well no longer be an issue.

Screw-cap reduction first came to light in the AWRI's closure studies, which commenced in 1999. "It can be argued that closing the bottle remains one of the greatest technical issues facing the wine industry," suggested lead authors Peter Godden and Leigh Francis in the introduction to the report. "The winemaker can control many aspects of wine production to create a wine suitable for the marketplace, and yet there can be an unpredictable incidence of problems once the wine is bottled, due in large part to the properties of the closures used."

The same wine, a respectable Clare Valley Semillon, was bottled using fourteen different closures and followed with regular chemical and sensory analysis. The results after twenty-one months in bottle (published in 2001) showed that while the screw-capped wine kept fruit freshness and retained free SO_2 the best of all the closures, it also suffered from a sensory defect described by the expert tasters as "rubber/struck flint." This was a surprising finding and caused a great deal of head scratching and anxiety within the trade. Shortly after publication, Godden had this to say about it:

> We are very confident that the "rubber-like" character is not a taint, but is an unwelcome modification due to chemically reduced sulfur, as a result of lack of oxygen. However, it is certainly an important character in screw-cap-closed wine, and we have highlighted its existence to avoid mass bottling of wine under extremely anaerobic conditions, which might then develop a similar character somewhere in the future.

This "reduction" was still evident five years post-bottling in the Semillon used in the trial.

The AWRI results raised a number of questions. What is the explanation for this reduction? Was the problem specific to this wine? How much of an issue is it with real-world wines being drunk by consumers? And what does it suggest about the role of the closure in wine development?

The prevailing view at the time was that the ideal closure would be one that seals hermetically, allowing no oxygen transmission at all. But a further trial from the AWRI seemed to indicate that an anaerobic closure might be entirely unsuitable for wine. This trial involved comparing a Chardonnay sealed three different ways: with cork, with screw cap, and hermetically sealed in a glass ampoule. The Chardonnay underwent some development in all three cases, but with the screw cap there was a bit of reduction and with the ampoule there was a lot. Another study, this time looking at a Penfolds Bin 389 red wine—sealed with synthetic cork, natural cork, and screw cap—also encountered some reduction in the screw-capped bottle. One of the important observations from this trial, though, is that it shows that wine doesn't need oxygen transmission through the closure for it to develop. The Chardonnay in the ampoule did show development: it wasn't locked in time.

We need to pause here for a technical aside. The screw cap itself is just a means for holding a liner in apposition to the rim of the bottle. It is the properties of this liner that determine the oxygen transmission levels of the closure. Until 2013 there were just two different liners available for wine. The first, and most widely used, is called "tin–Saran." This consists of a Saran backing with a metal layer (usually tin, but it can be aluminum) that is covered by a thin layer of PVDC, which is in contact with the wine. This metal liner allows very little oxygen transmission at all. It is the liner used almost universally in Australia and New Zealand. In the United States and Europe it is still the most widely used liner, but you are also likely to encounter the alternative liner, known as "Saranex only," which consists solely of Saranex. The latter allows more oxygen transmission and is not implicated in the screw-cap reduction story. (In 2013, a new set of five liners with a range of oxygen transmission levels were introduced by Alcan, but these are not yet used widely enough that I can comment on their performance.)

Back to the issue of reduction. What is happening here? It all has to do with the issue of sulfur compound chemistry. As we have discussed in this chapter, during fermentation, yeasts can produce VSCs such as sulfides and mercaptans. So why is reduction a problem that has been associated by some with screw-cap use? It has to do with a concept known as *redox potential.* This is a measure of how oxidative or reductive a system, such as a wine in barrel or bottle, is. It is measured in millivolts (mV)—the higher the reading, the less reductive. Typically, an aerated red wine will have a redox potential of 400–450 mV, whereas storage in the absence of air for some time will reduce this to 200–250 mV. If levels get as low as 150 mV, there is a danger that reduction problems can occur. Exposure to oxygen through winemaking practices such as racking, topping up barrels, and filtering increases the level of dissolved oxygen in the wine and increases the redox potential, which will then return to 200–300 mV. This redox level will change much more rapidly in white wines than in reds, because red wines have a higher concentration of phenolic compounds such as tannins that are able to interact with oxygen and act as buffers. Another variable here is the level of free SO_2 in the wine, which will act protectively by reacting with the products of oxidation. Yeast lees also scavenge oxygen and protect the wine in a similar fashion, helping to lower the redox potential and create a more reductive environment. In modern winemaking, reductive conditions are encouraged: the protection of wines from oxygen by the use of stainless steel tanks and inert gases helps to preserve fresh-fruit characters. These reductive conditions—in which oxygen is more or less excluded—can also favor the development of smelly forms of sulfur compounds.

After bottling, the redox state of the wine will be influenced by a number of factors, including the state of the wine at bottling, the free SO_2 levels, the oxygen pickup during the bottling procedure, headspace extent and composition (air or inert gas), and the oxygen transmission by the closure. As we've seen, "reduction" seems to be a problem in these sorts of analytical studies involving metal-lined screw caps, and the obvious explanation is that the low-redox environment of the screw-cap-sealed wine is causing some unwanted sulfur chemistry to occur, with sulfur compounds shifting from a less smelly (and thus unnoticed) form to a more smelly (and thus noticeable), more reduced form. (This is assuming the wine is bottled clean, of course.)

What are we to make of "screw-cap reduction"? Is it a real-world problem on a par with cork taint, or is it just a minor technical problem—a teething issue that just needs a bit of tweaking? The widespread adoption of screw caps by the Australian and New Zealand wine industries with very few reported problems suggests the latter may be the case. Or is it one of those issues where chemical analysis demonstrated a problem, but in terms of the actual taste of the wine, it's something that will only be picked up by a trained sensory panel who are looking for it?

The view of some winemakers is that proper preparation of wine before bottling, and then bottling with lower SO_2 levels— and perhaps allowing a little bit of oxygen pickup—will prevent any reduction issues after bottling. Typically, winemakers who are concerned about reductive tendencies in a particular wine will do a copper fining trial; many actually do a prophylactic addition of copper, although there is now good evidence that late additions of copper can make things worse. How does copper fining work? Copper is oxidative and will preferentially oxidize the smelly short-chain thiols and the sulfides. However, it is unable to deal with any disulfides present. The idea is that winemakers do a fining trial, adding just enough copper that it deals with the smelly compounds without having a negative effect on the wine (for example, by targeting the polyfunctional thiols, which can have a positive quality impact).

Is the issue of mercaptans in screw-capped wines problematic enough that some caution should be exercised in the use of the tin–Saran liner? This is a controversial question. Ph.D. chemist Alan Limmer, who set up the Stonecroft winery in New Zealand's Hawkes Bay (he's since sold it) was for a while very vocal on this issue. In particular, Limmer has pointed out that screw-cap reduction is not a problem that can be completely eliminated by better winemaking, as many have claimed. "In essence we are talking about thiol accumulation, post-bottling, from complex sulfides which do not respond to pre-bottling copper treatment," he claims, in response to the assertion that fining with copper removes reduction defects. "This reaction occurs to all wines containing the appropriate precursors, irrespective of closure type. But the varying levels of oxygen ingress between closures lead to significantly different outcomes from a sensory point of view."

Limmer's explanation of screw-cap reduction is that sulfides present in the wine at bottling necessitate a very small level of oxygen ingress through the closure; otherwise they can become reduced to thiols. Because sulfides are less smelly, it is possible for a wine that is clean at bottling to taste reduced after bottling if the closure doesn't permit enough oxygen ingress. So the use of a closure, such as cork, which does allow a little oxygen ingress (but not too much) is a necessary concession to the vagaries of sulfur chemistry. Of course, we'd rather not have the sulfides in the wine at all, which would then avoid problems with reduction to mercaptans at a later stage. But, as Limmer points out,

> Controlling ferments to not produce the complex sulfides is beyond our means currently. This sulfide behavior of the ferment is more controlled by the yeast genetics than the winemaker. It is not the

winemaker's fault these compounds exist in the wine at bottling. We can minimize it to some extent by providing optimum nutrient conditions for the ferment, and employing some specific winemaking regimes. But the research tells us this only has a slight impact on the complex sulfide pattern produced by the yeast.

Others think that care taken during winemaking, and particularly at bottling, can significantly reduce the risk of any reduction. Wise counsel would be that winemakers intending to use tin-lined screw caps should first of all ensure they have clean, healthy ferments. Then they should be in control of bottling parameters. It is important to get the wine clean before bottling, without any trace of mercaptan or disulfide. A healthy ferment should be the first priority. When it comes to bottling, it is not advisable to use free SO_2 levels that are a little lower than those used with other closures, as some have advocated: the larger headspace in a screw-capped bottle means that there isn't latitude for reducing SO_2 levels, even though the low oxygen transmission rate will help these levels remain higher longer. It should be emphasized that allowing more oxygen pickup or leaving a larger headspace of air does not counter post-bottling reduction, but rather results in a bit of oxidation. And as we have discussed, copper fining can help in some circumstances: it certainly gets rid of mercaptans, but it doesn't eliminate disulfides, which can, as we have seen, revert to mercaptans in a low-redox environment.

The extent of screw-cap reduction in the real world is currently unclear. On one level, the fact that around 95 percent of New Zealand wines and some 80 percent of Australian wines are sealed with tin–Saran screw caps—and these wines are commercially successful, with few consumer dislike issues—is evidence that the problem isn't a major one. It should be borne in mind that cork taint irredeemably ruins bottles that it affects, whereas very few consumers will have a problem with low-level mercaptans in their wines. I doubt that most of the wine trade would spot this as a problem in all but the most extreme cases, so it is unfair to equate it with the very well-recognized problem of cork taint. Having said this, though, screw-cap-sealed wines affected by mercaptans should be a major concern for winemakers because the closure is modifying the flavor of the wine, which is emphatically not reaching the consumer "the way the winemaker intended." It would be dangerously complacent for the industry to take the view that if the consumer doesn't notice it, then it doesn't matter.

A recent report[4] from Eric Wilkes of the AWRI has looked at nine years' worth of data from the International Wine Challenge, one of the world's best-judged and largest blind tasting competitions (disclaimer: I am one of the six cochairs of this competition). For each of those nine years, any wine declared faulty by one of the twenty or so tasting panels was sent to the faults clinic. There, until 2017, Sam Harrop MW was responsible for checking each "faulty" bottle, and assigning it to one of several fault categories, or declaring it not faulty. The database of faults from a sample of more than a hundred thousand bottles from around the world has been examined by the AWRI. Over this period, they found that the rate of rejection for reductive characters was exactly the same for cork-sealed and screw-cap-sealed bottles, at 0.81 percent. Wilkes concluded that "the wine's intrinsic nature can play a much greater role in the development of reductive issues, with the closure modulating, not defining, the outcome." The AWRI looked at the development of the VSC methanethiol in the same wine sealed with nine different closures and found that after two years in bottle, the closure was relatively insignificant in affecting the methanethiol level in the wine. Wilkes concludes that VSC development is dependent on a range of issues, and he lists four as examples: the concentration of metal ions such as copper; the nutritional status of the must; the choice of yeast used; and the history of oxygen exposure of both the must and the wine.

How do you spot low-level mercaptans? "They impact from an organoleptic perspective towards the end of the palate," claims Limmer, "imparting a 'mineral' or bitter/hard/astringent aspect. This has the appearance of shortening or closing up the palate, so the wine does not display a fine, fresh, long finish, but ends abruptly, and somewhat harshly."

I asked Maurizio Ugliano whether a bit of oxygen transmission through the closure is needed to avoid reduction issues. "That depends on the wine," he responded. "Even under natural cork you can see wines developing reduction." He added that

> reduction seems to show in bottles between six and eighteen months: this seems to be a critical time for reduction. In that moment, all the other players of oxygen, excluding oxygen transmission through the closure, are effectively already gone from the picture. The oxygen from bottling has been consumed; the oxygen from the body of the closure has been expelled and consumed. In that phase you will probably benefit from a little oxygen ingress. When we look at natural cork it is always a bit frustrating from a scientific point of view because the material is so variable. We tend to call a good cork—a high-grade cork—the one with incredibly low permeability. Within the same lot we observe a big range of variation, and we say that the bottles that will keep well are the ones where the cork seal is tighter. But we don't know this for sure. It might be that the ones that keep well are those that are sort of tight but not super-tight. No one has looked at this. Maybe natural cork producers have, but they don't disclose this information because they haven't been able to control this property of their closures yet.

While the development of sulfur-like odors in wine is normally best avoided, there are some circumstances where they can contribute something positive. New Zealand winemaker James Healey points out some of these:

> In Champagne the bready/brioche character from aging for a period on lees is a result of a certain type of reduction in association with autolysis and liberation of the contents of yeast cells into the wine. The reductive characters from fermentation of Chardonnay juice containing highish solid concentrations result in accentuated nuttiness and improved texture after aging on lees for some time.

Leigh Francis agrees that reduced characters aren't always negative:

> Overall, as always with flavor chemistry and sensory properties, it is hard to be too definitive about negative/positive. A small amount of a particular character in a wine that has other fairly strong aroma attributes will likely be accepted and liked. It's when the aroma dominates that the [reduced sulfur] compounds could be considered negative, but this is probably the case with any aroma you can think of: too much of a good thing can be too overwhelming and make the wine too simple and not attractive to drink much of. For sulfur compounds in general it does seem, however, that when they're at very high concentrations an unpleasant note becomes evident, no matter how pleasant they seem at lower levels, which is not the case for many other flavor compounds. It is likely that hydrogen sulfide will be negative no matter what level.

Dominique Delteil gives two examples of how sulfur characters can be positive according to their context:

> First, a very ripe Languedoc Syrah macerated to reach liquorice aromas, and then aged in oak. In that wine, hints of "burnt match" could be very interesting from a sensory point of view. They will match the ripe fruit/vanilla style. Most wine drinkers will

appreciate that, because those aromas are in a very sweet aromatic environment, so they won't express as dominant. Second, a cool-climate unripe Cabernet Sauvignon. Let's suppose that this wine has exactly (chemically speaking) the same amount of the sulfur compounds that gave the interesting light "burnt match" in the above Syrah. In that wine those chemicals will give a different sensation that the same taster will translate as "leek," "green bean," and eventually "garlic."

Delteil gives two explanations, from a sensory and a chemical perspective:

Sensory answer: the same sensation (the molecules reaching the sensory bulb in the palate cavity) will produce different perception (neuro-sensorial unconscious feeling) and finally a different translation (the conscious expression, such as the pronounced word "garlic") according to the other compounds reaching the sensory bulb at the same time. This phenomenon is very well known in cooking. So some vegetal character in the unripe Cabernet will emphasize the sensation and translation. On the contrary, the ripe aromas of the Syrah make more acceptable and even interesting the same amount of chemical compounds. Chemical answer: recently there has been significant progress in understanding the chemistry of macromolecules in wine, particularly with the work carried out in the INRA in Montpellier by Professor Moutounet and his team. An interaction has been identified (nonclassical chemical links between molecules) between volatile compounds and some polysaccharides from the grape, the yeast, or the lactic acid bacteria. It is also known now that ripe grapes release more macromolecules into the wine. So in our examples, maybe there was the same amount of sulfur compounds (from a classical analytical chemistry point of view) but the volatilities were different because of a higher macromolecule concentration in our ripe Syrah.

Delteil thinks that with the sorts of wines he is making in the Mediterranean regions, from very ripe grapes, "it is interesting to manage sulfur characters closer to the razor edge, once we are sure that we are managing the basic sulfur off-flavors risks." Oxygen is a useful tool in this sort of manipulation.

Once one gets the first level of security with yeast, nutrients, and so on, with a lower amount of oxygen one can play around with the "burnt match" character. Working this way one also helps preserve native fruit characters. So, there is a double effect: hints of burnt match with rich fresher fruit. If the wine is backed with very rich ripe fruit, it is a style change that can be attractive. In hot-climate areas, it recalls the good characters of cooler areas (when they reach ripening!). It is trendy today not to push too far the natural ripe Mediterranean style. Oak management is also a tool to complement ripeness with mineral/smoky/fresh-fruit characters.

Sam Harrop has a fascinating idea, albeit one that may prove difficult to test. In chemical terms, minerality is an ill-defined quality in wine, though when it does occur it is commonly explained as being a terroir character. But what if it is actually a consequence of reduction, caused by a combination of VSCs at low levels? "Wines from many of the best wine regions in France show mineral/reductive qualities," says Harrop. "Perhaps these qualities are derived in the winery and not the vineyard."

"I do believe that minerality and reduction are related," says Healey. He explains:

> It could be a result of struggling ferments coupled with nutrient deficiency/vine stress but I don't think that this is why great white Burgundy or Riesling achieve this character. I think these wines derive this character because the producers understand how to get it from their vines and vinifications. I suppose that someone could fluke it from time to time, but there are many great producers that consistently hit the nail year after year.

Delteil agrees that flavors from sulfur compounds are often misidentified as terroir characters. He recounts his experience with a client in Friuli. "According to the commercial manager, the flinty character was too high in the wine even though they were applying classical prevention practices." Delteil looked to see how the flintiness could be reduced and found that the best method was through amplifying the ripe-grape character.

> It was a classical pendulum effect between ripe fruit and sulfur, and we now have an accepted level of flint hints for the market goal. I personally think that excessive sulfur characters are too often presented as a terroir expression (so nobody can say a word about it because it's terroir!) although they [represent] a non-understanding of the risks created by a situation and [by] the winemaker. And when one applies a better-adapted process, that famous terroir appears to be a luscious fruit source!

How can the negative effects of sulfur compounds be managed? "By prevention," says Delteil. "For prevention, a minimum knowledge of the phenomenon is necessary." He explains the good practice he tries to develop with the wineries he works with:

> Sulfur compounds are produced by the yeast, either during its life or after its death: this is 99 percent of sulfur flavors. Then, those compounds are chemically extremely reactive. So, what we identify with a word such as "garlic" comes from yeast native molecules (molecules liberated by the yeast in the chemical form they have when they reach our sensory bulb) and from sulfur compounds that are produced through different chemical reactions during fermentation and aging. But almost everything comes from the yeast, so prevention is based on the yeast.

He adds that avoiding the production of excessive sulfur compounds is a complex matter:

> The key point is the yeast strain. There are huge differences between the different yeasts. That's true among the hundreds

of selected enological natural yeasts available today, and also among the indigenous yeasts. This is then amplified by the yeast nutrition, the second key point. The higher the sugar in the juice, the lower the natural content in complex nitrogen compounds (particularly amino acids), the higher the yeast stress and higher the risk of sulfur compounds in excess. Those conditions are typically found in the Mediterranean areas. Once the yeast strain and the nutrition are OK, oxygen will be an extra tool for the winemaker. If the first two key points are not managed, it is hazardous to manage the problem just with oxygen. Why? Stressed yeast cells produce sulfur compounds continually, and "high oxygen" winemaking processes add oxygen once a day in reds and once or twice during the whole fermentation in white or rosé. So the oxygen added arrives to find some already-stabilized sulfur compounds. The third key point is yeast management during aging. Once a winemaker has made a fermentation without a sulfur problem, he must manage the risk due to dead yeast. Many practices are consistent. If one keeps a certain level of dead yeast (we call them light lees), it is recommended that they should be stirred regularly into the wine to avoid reductive zones in the tank or the barrel. Here *reductive* is used in its proper physico-chemical sense. This movement is the reason for the traditional stirring *(bâtonnage)* during aging with lees. The right amount of oxygen is also important, either through the stirring or through direct managed injections.

So, how should winemakers enhance the positive effects of sulfur compounds? "They should amplify the other positive characters in the wine," says Delteil,

that is, ripe aromas (fruity, spicy, vanilla, etc., according to the grape, the place, the style goals, the market goals) and round mouthfeel sensations. Among ripe aromas, sulfur flavors will express as mineral characters and in mouth they won't provoke too much dryness and bitterness in the aftertaste. Why talk about mouthfeel? Some common sense: volatile compounds that are aggressive to the olfactive bulb through ortho-olfaction (direct

TABLE 3

Some of the Key Volatile Sulfur Compounds in Wine

Name[a]	Sensory descriptor	Perception threshold	Comments
Hydrogen sulfide (H₂S)	Rotten eggs, drains	1 mg/L	What we normally think of as reduction. Produced by yeasts during fermentation in varying amounts.
Dimethyl sulfide (DMS)	Canned corn, cooked cabbage, asparagus	25 µg/L	Enhances fruity flavors in young red wines and can contribute truffle characters to older wines.
3-Mercaptohexyl acetate (3MHA) [3-sulfanylhexyl acetate]	Grapefruit zest, passionfruit (*R* enantiomer); more herbaceous, boxwood (*S* enantiomer)	9 ng/L (*R*); 2.5 ng/L (*S*)	Very important in the fruity aroma of Marlborough Sauvignon Blanc. During aging of wine, this hydrolyzes to 3MH.
3-Mercaptohexan-1-ol (3MH) [3-sulfanylhexan-1-ol]	Passionfruit (*S* enantiomer); grapefruit (*R* enantiomer)	60 ng/L (*S*); 50 ng/L (*R*)	Always present in Sauvignon Blanc, at concentrations ranging from several hundred ng/L to as high as mg/L. Wines with highest levels of 3MH tend to have the highest levels of 3MHA.

(continued)

TABLE 3
(continued)

Name[a]	Sensory descriptor	Perception threshold	Comments
4-Mercapto-4-methylpentan-2-one (4MMP) [4-methyl-4-sulfanylpentan-2-one]	Box tree, broom	0.8 ng/L	Present at up to 100 ng/L in fresh box leaves; can be found at up to 40 ng/L in some Sauvignon Blancs.
3-Mercapto-3-methylbutan-1-ol (3MMB)	Cooked leeks	1,500 ng/L	Rarely found in wine above perception threshold.
4-Methyl-4-mercaptopentan-2-ol (4MMPOH)	Citrus zest	55 ng/L (20 ng/L in water)	
2-Furanmethanethiol (also known as 2-furfurylthiol or 2-furfurylmethyl mercaptan)	Roasted coffee	0.4 ng/L	Identified in sweet whites from Petit Manseng variety and red Bordeaux wines and has been found in toasted oak. Also found in Champagne aroma.
Ethyl-3-mercaptoproprionate	Meaty		Found in the aroma of Champagne.
4-Methyl-4-mercaptopentan-2-ol	Citrus zest	55 ng/L	Rarely found in wine above perception threshold.

Methanethiol (methyl mercaptan)	Rotten cabbage, stagnant water	1.5 ng/L	
Ethanethiol (= ethyl mercaptan)	Rotten onion, burnt rubber at threshold levels; skunky or fecal at higher levels	1.1 ng/L	
2-Mercaptoethanol	Barnyard		
Ethanedithiol	Rubber, rotten cabbage		
Benzenemethanethiol (also known as phenylmethanethiol and benzylmercaptan)	Gunflint, flint, struck match, smoky	0.3 ng/L	Potentially responsible for reductive aromas in some wines. Found as a component of Champagne aroma.

[a] Terminology can differ. For example, *mercapto* is sometimes interchanged with *sulfanyl* in these names. Here, I have chosen to use the most widely adopted name for each of the thiols, which is currently the *mercapto* version. Technically, however, the correct name (according to the International Union of Pure and Applied Chemistry) is the *sulfanyl* one, so I have given this in square brackets in a few instances, although this terminology is not yet widely used in the literature (however, that could change over the life span of this book).

smell, versus retro-olfaction) are not 100 percent volatile. Most of the compounds (in quantity) stay in solution in the wine (at tasting temperature) and so will come into contact with the mouth, and will come across as aggressive there just as they are in the olfactive bulb. That impact of sulfur compounds on mouthfeel is not often known and integrated in winemaking although it is very important for consumers.

In conclusion, reduction is another one of those truly interesting faults that can't really be called a fault. Instead, we need a more nuanced view of volatile sulfur compounds, recognizing that context and concentration are important. Managing these compounds well is going to enhance wine quality, but they also have the potential to reduce quality.

CHAPTER SEVEN

Musty Taints: Cork Taint and Its Relatives

- **What is it?** A range of musty-smelling taints that affect an annoyingly high proportion of wines.
- **What is its flavor impact?** Wines smell musty: in the worst-case scenario, the smell is immediately and obviously off-putting. But in other cases it's a marginal taint, with diminished aromas and a faint mustiness.
- **What causes it?** Musty taints in wine have a number of causes. Often it is the microbial contamination of cork, but it can also be from the winery environment. There are a number of compounds implicated in this.
- **Is it always bad?** Yes, if it's detectable.
- **How can it be prevented?** Once a wine is contaminated, it's too late.
- **How common is it?** Estimates are that around 2–5 percent of wines sealed with corks are affected, but some of the reported rates in some countries were much higher in the past.

In our discussion of wine faults, we have noted several that can actually be positive in the right amount. There is one fault, however, to which that caveat does not apply. This is musty taint, most commonly (but not exclusively) imparted to wine by fault compounds present in contaminated corks. When it's present, it's always a fault.

Cork's struggles with taint are well documented. The major compound responsible for musty taints from cork is 2,4,6-trichloroanisole (TCA), which is formed in cork bark by the chemical combination of phenolic compounds with chlorine. There are also other compounds that can cause musty taints, such as geosmin (threshold of 25 ng/L), 1-octen-3-ol (threshold of 20 µg/L), 1-octen-3-one (threshold of 20 ng/L), 2-methylisoborneol (threshold of 30 ng/L), and 2-methoxy-3,5-dimethylpyrazine (threshold of 2.1 ng/L). But it is TCA that is largely responsible. The phenolic compounds in TCA are present as a result of the breakdown of lignin, which is the hard substance naturally occurring in tree bark. The chlorine comes from the environment. It is widely accepted that the major source of environmental chlorine in cork oak forests are organochlorine insecticides that were widely used from the 1950s to the 1980s. Even though they are no longer used, chlorine residues are still present in the soil at the base of the trees and will remain there for some time.

We're incredibly sensitive to TCA and its chemical relatives and can detect them at very low concentrations. Most people can spot TCA at a concentration of around 5 ng/L (which is the same as five parts per trillion), although this depends on the wine context and the sensitivity of the individual: it is easier to spot tainted whites than heavy reds. This corresponds to the equivalent of a few drops in an Olympic-size slimming pool. It's likely that the ability to spot TCA is adaptive, because the chemical indicates the presence of fungi such as molds in food, which could present a health hazard (though TCA itself, at the levels found in tainted wine, is harmless). Some people can detect TCA at concentrations as low as 2 ng/L; others don't recognize it at 10 ng/L. A few people can't smell it at all (they are anosmic to TCA).

This makes life very hard for the cork industry. There's no easy way to tell a good cork from a bad one visually, so winemakers have either had to resign themselves to losing a certain percentage of the wines they seal with cork to taint or switch to cork alternatives such as screw caps and synthetic corks. Many winemakers choose to remain with cork. The good news for them is that the cork industry is responding to criticism and doing something about natural cork quality, trying to understand the causes of TCA and also to devise ways of removing it, as well as developing methods to test individual corks for TCA. Some of the solutions are common across many cork companies; others are proprietary. In this chapter, we will look at the problem of musty taint and discuss exactly how much of it is down to the cork and what the other possible sources are. I will try to assess how much progress is being made and whether the steps that are being taken are likely to result in a significant reduction in the number of tainted bottles—and thus breathe a new lease on life into cork as a wine bottle closure.

WHEN CORK TAINT WAS FIRST OBSERVED

Although the wine industry was aware of musty taints from affected corks for a long time, it wasn't until the early 1980s that Swiss scientist Hans Tanner and his team published research that identified TCA as the main culprit in cork taint. Since then, a number of other musty-smelling compounds have been identified in wine, some associated with corks and others associated with winery taints, for example from treated wood in winery structures.

Biologically, these haloanisoles are commonly produced by microbes in a defensive reaction against a group of potentially toxic compounds called *halophenols*. This biochemical defensive reaction is called *biomethylation*, and it is most common in filamentous fungi. Chlorophenols and bromophenols are commonly used as pesticides and fungicides, and the fungi respond to them by turning them into nontoxic haloanisoles, which represents a sort of survival mechanism. One source of such halophenols is in the hypochlorite treatment that used to be a cleaning step in cork production (it is rarely used these days). But microbes can also produce TCA through other pathways. Many microbes can form phenols that are then chlorinated.

ESTIMATES OF THE INCIDENCE OF CORK TAINT

How common is cork taint? The first large, systematic survey was carried out in the United Kingdom by the Wine and Spirit Association (WSA). The "WSA Musty Flavour Defects in Wine in the UK" survey involved a consortium of eighteen companies, including retailers, producers, wholesalers, and stopper manufacturers. Over the course of twelve months, from January 2001 to January 2002, data were collected on over thirteen thousand wines tasted by assessors in the contributing companies during the course of their work. The publication of the final report, in June 2002, provoked a storm of controversy, principally because the final quoted figure of verified musty taint prevalence was very low, at 0.7 percent. It turns out that the tainted bottles were verified only by sensory analysis; they were verified some time after opening (and oxidation masks cork taint); and the bottles were resealed with corks, which could have reabsorbed some of the taint compounds. For these reasons, the study was discredited.

AWRI Data

Once or twice a year, the AWRI runs a four-day course for potential wine-show judges, known as the Advanced Wine Assessment Course (AWAC). A large number of bottles from around the world are opened during these courses, and because of the scientifically rigorous approach applied, this represents perhaps the best-verified assessment of the incidence of TCA in cork-sealed wines. Participants taste in silence and then discuss their results. For a bottle to be regarded as TCA-affected, 15 percent of participants must have identified the taint during their assessment. There is backup to this sensory analysis in the form of chemical analysis: over the last three AWACs, all wines described as TCA-affected by the panel and then analyzed by gas chromatography–mass spectrometry have proved to be TCA-tainted.

During the three AWACs held immediately prior to June 2003, a total of 1,625 bottles sealed with cork were sampled, 6.46 percent of which showed TCA taint. If statistical confidence limits are applied, we can be 99 percent sure that if this sample is representative of all wines sealed with cork, the real rate of taint is between 5 and 8.2 percent. In fact, the sample here is skewed towards higher-priced wines, which likely would have been sealed with more expensive corks (though, it must be pointed out, there is no indication that taint rate bears any relationship to the price of the cork). Other interesting observations were that Australian wines were no more likely to be cork-tainted than those from France, for example, and that the taint rate was slightly higher in whites than in reds (suggesting that some low-level taint might have been more apparent in whites and went unnoticed in some reds). Data were collated but never published on subsequent AWACs up until 2007, and the taint rates were similarly high.

International Wine Challenge Results

Each year, the International Wine Challenge is held in London. An enormous number of bottles are opened and tasted systematically by panels made up largely of experienced tasters. Although a tally of cork-tainted bottles had been kept in previous years—in 2001 it was 6 percent, and in 2002 it was 4.6 percent—in 2003 all cases of suspected mustiness were verified as cork taint by a "superjuror." The results were that of 11,033 bottles sealed with natural corks, 4.9 percent were considered to be cork-tainted. A further 2.79 percent were faulty for other reasons. This figure tallies well with results from other surveys. From 2005 on, there was a dedicated faults clinic at the International Wine Challenge. Over the five years from 2006 to 2010, the average rate of cork taint was 2.8 percent (individual years: 2.8, 3.3, 3, 3.2, and 1.9 percent). The weakness of this sort of sampling is that it is likely to throw up false positives and that low-level TCA contamination will be missed in some cases. Although there is no chemical analysis of bottles judged to be affected, the scale of the sampling is impressive enough to mean that these are useful results, and most wine-trade tasters are pretty good at spotting cork taint.

Wine Spectator *Data*

Influential U.S. publication the *Wine Spectator* keeps a tally of cork-tainted wines. Its California editor and staff taster, James Laube, reported that of the 3,269 California wines tasted in the magazine's office in 2012, 3.7 percent were cork-tainted. He adds that this is the lowest percentage seen yet, down from 3.8 percent in 2011 and a high of 9.5 percent in 2007.

Decanter World Wine Awards

According to judge Andrew Jefford, in the 2012 Decanter World Wine Awards, some 3.3 percent of the 14,120 entries were dismissed as TCA-spoiled. However, 10 percent of those wines turned out to be either screw-capped or non-cork-stoppered, so there may have been some false positives. Judges can sometimes see cork taint where there is none, or confuse other faults with cork taint. Also, some musty taints aren't caused by corks, as I will discuss below.

DEALING WITH MUSTY TAINT IN CORKS

There are two rather different, yet complementary, approaches to dealing with TCA and related compounds in corks. The first is to use quality-control measures to try to prevent contaminated cork from being turned into closures that then leave the factory. The second is to assume that some TCA may be present, and to then remove it by some sort of extractive or washing method—the curative approach. Put both strategies together, and substantial reductions can be obtained even if either strategy is not 100 percent effective alone.

Perhaps the most striking example of the curative approach is that employed by French company Oeneo in the production of their DIAM closure. This involves the use of a technology already employed by the perfume and food industries, "supercritical point carbon dioxide washing." Its use in treating wine cork was devised by Oeneo (who were at this stage called Sabaté) in the late 1990s in conjunction with the Supercritical Fluids and Membranes laboratory of France's CEA (Commissariat à l'Energie Atomique). Sabaté had experienced terrible taint problems with their Altec technical cork, which was a novel product that combined tiny cork granules with synthetic microspheres to make a durable, functional natural-cork-based closure—albeit one where any TCA present in batches of cork was shared out equally among all the closures!

Supercritical carbon dioxide—used to remove caffeine from coffee and to extract aromas for perfumes—is quite hard to understand for the nonscientist. If you pressurize a gas, at a certain point it becomes a liquid. If you then juggle the parameters of pressure and temperature, at a specific combination of these—known as the critical point—the interface between the two disappears, and you then have the penetration power of a gas and the extraction power of a liquid. For carbon dioxide this point is at 31.1°C and 73 bars of pressure. Sabaté found that this novel technology actually worked and removed all the TCA from the starting material, ground-up fragments of cork. Thus, the new generation of Altecs was born: the first cork-based closures that were completely free from the risk of musty taint. Sabaté changed its name to Oeneo, and the new taint-free Altecs, named DIAM, went into production at a brand-new factory in Spain at San Vicente De Alcántara, on the border with Portugal. So far, DIAM closures have been widely adopted and no incidences of musty taint have been seen in practice.

Bruno de Saizieu, sales director of DIAM, is upbeat about how well these taint-free microagglomerate technical corks are performing. "People are putting DIAM on more and more top-level wines," he says. "Forty percent of Grand Cru Burgundy are now under DIAM. When you have top wines under DIAM, it's easier to convince other people to go there." In 2016 they sold 1.5 billion closures. "Things are going fast and we are thinking of a new supercritical plant." Their third factory will be full in the next two years (they have two in Spain and one in France so far). A new facility will be a big investment, costing around €30 million. The sparkling-wine equivalet, Mytik DIAM, is being adopted by leading Champagne houses such as Moët et Chandon.

DIAM represents one extreme in the fight against taint: take what might well be contaminated material and clean it so thoroughly that all taint is eradicated. It is so effective that although the starting material—inexpensive waste off-cuts of cork— would seem particularly unpromising, the cleaning process eliminates the taints.

Steam-based treatments have become popular among cork manufacturers, and the success of DIAM has led to a raft of new "microagglomerate" corks. These closures, which have a more sophisticated appearance than traditional agglomerates, with a finer grain from the smaller cork particles used to form them, are a huge TCA risk unless the particles are somehow cleaned, and steam is a relatively inexpensive way of doing so. But if a sophisticated steam method, such as Amorim's ROSA process, can remove around 80 percent of releasable TCA, then the starting point is highly significant. Thus, a combinatorial approach that brings together several preventive steps in the journey from bark to finished closure, combined with a curative method such as steam cleaning, and then finished off with advanced quality-control measures such as gas chromatography analysis, will mean that far fewer tainted corks and other closures will leave the factories.

Amorim is the world's largest cork-producing company, and the changes it has implemented over recent years are impressive in their scope. First, the freshly harvested cork is laid out to season on concrete rather than bare earth. At their cork processing plant in Ponte do Sur there is an enormous area, the size of a few football fields, laid with concrete on which the cork bales are piled in large stacks. Álvaro Coelho and Irmãos (known as ACI in the United States) have a similar facility.

The next stage in cork production is boiling the planks, which in the past was a potential source of contamination because repeated batches of bark were all boiled in the same water, in open pits. Amorim now use a system where the boiling water is replaced, and the volatiles are removed during the process (which they call Convex, for "continuous volatile extraction"). Other companies have changed their boiling systems also.

The ROSA process, Amorim's proprietal steam-cleaning step, is now applied to all granules used in production of Twin-Top, Neutrocork, and Advantec closures. Independent verification shows that it reduces TCA levels in the granules by around 80 percent. The typical starting point for cork used for making granules is now 2–4 ng/L TCA, and the facilities producing these granules now have an upper limit for accepting bales of cork of 8–9 g/L TCA. Amorim has also developed a separate system, called ROSA Evolution, for treating natural corks: the difficulty has been adapting the system so that TCA is removed but the corks maintain their physical integrity, but by making the treatment step longer and more gentle they have achieved this.

Finally, there is laboratory analysis. Amorim has gas chromatography–mass spectrometry and gas chromatography–electron capture machines, which can look for TCA down to a detection limit of 0.5 ng/L. In 2016, Amorim announced that for some high-end natural corks, they have the capacity to test each cork individually for TCA. This is called NDtech, and it makes use of new, faster gas chromatography technology that delivers results in just seconds, as opposed to the fifteen minutes that other technology takes. This makes feasible individualized quality-control screening where each cork is tested and given a nondetectable-TCA guarantee (a level below 0.5 ng/L). Although it makes already expensive natural cork even pricier, for high-end wines it is justifiable. Amorim expected to have produced fifty million of these guaranteed clean corks in 2016. This is an exciting development for those who like the way wines age under cork but who don't want to risk taint and who find the appearance of microagglomerates unsatisfying.

WINERY CONTAMINATION

In addition to TCA, other haloanisoles have been implicated in musty taints in wines. Three are byproducts of the microbial degradation of wood preservatives and fire retardants: 2,3,4,6-tetrachloroanisole (TeCA), pentachloroanisole (PCA), and 2,4,6-tribromoanisole (TBA).

The first report of musty taint in wine caused by the winery environment was as recent as 2004, when Pascal Chatonnet and colleagues at Laboratoire Excell examined three French wineries and found TBA inside them at high enough concentrations to taint the wine.[1] This was produced by microbial degradation of the flame retardant and fungicide tribromophenol, which had been used to treat wood (it's also commonly used to treat plastics and cardboard). In one cellar, Chatonnet found that the wooden racks had 2,185 ng of TBA per gram of wood, and in one tested barrel of wine the levels were 38 ng/L, well above the detection threshold for TBA, which is 3.4 ng/L. Formed by the biomethylation of tribromophenol by microorganisms such as filamentous fungi, TBA is a defense mechanism for the microbes: tribromophenol is toxic, while the haloanisoles such as TBA are not. In wineries there are many potential sources of tribromophenol, including wood pallets, catwalks, barrel chocks, plywood, wooden rafters and beams, hoses, plastics, filter pads, fining agents, and packaging materials. Also, wineries like to keep cellars humid to avoid loss of wine from barrels through evaporation, which encourages the growth of fungi.

A number of high-profile wineries have had problems with TBA contamination. In 2007, leading Chilean winery Errázuriz had an issue with some of the wooden sectors of their Panquehue winery, when a particular wine consistently showed TBA levels of 4.5 ng/L, which is just above the detection threshold. In June 2003, James Laube identified musty taints in the leading Sonoma Valley winery Hanzell's 1999 Pinot Noir and 2000 Chardonnay. The taint was only slight, but it was enough to cause the withdrawal of these wines from the market, although later Hanzell decided to sell the wines after their own tests with consumers and industry professionals convinced them that the taint wasn't significant. It was attributed to Hanzell's practice of using chlorine-based products to clean the cellars twice a year. Tests by ETS laboratories showed some TCA in these wines, but this was before Chatonnet's publication implicating TBA in winery contamination, which may have also been a factor. The following year, Laube outed another California winery, Chateau

Montelena, for the same problem. Tests showed TCA levels in the wines that were very low—at or below detection threshold.

How often is TBA a source of musty taint compared with TCA? In Australia over the period 1999–2009, AWRI Commercial Services analyzed over two thousand wines for musty taints. They found 861 positive cases of TCA taint and 109 positive cases of TBA taint, which suggests that TBA is more common than we might think. But a caveat has to be added here: this corresponds with a growing use of screw caps in Australia, so there would have been relatively fewer incidences of cork-caused taint because of this.

CONTAMINATED BARRELS

In 2010, Chatonnet and colleagues published a paper on another source of musty taint in wines: oak barrels.[2] Stavewood for barrels is produced by splitting (for French oak) or sawing (for American oak) oak logs. The trees are felled in the autumn and the stavewood is prepared the following summer. It's stored in piles, in the open air, and is rained on and/or sprayed with water to leach out undesirable flavor compounds. Staves are typically seasoned for two or three years, and then if their moisture content isn't just right, the process may be finished off in kilns. Chatonnet and colleagues looked at a Tempranillo from Rioja, 2007 vintage. The wine was being aged in 225 L barrels made from French and American oak, and after three months in barrel some wines from a specific cooperage were showing signs of musty taint while others were fine. In all, four out of forty barrels were tainted. They took apart the worst-affected barrel and looked at individual staves. The contamination was from just one stave that was part of the end of the barrel (untoasted). This showed levels of 6 ng/g of TCA and 8.5 ng/g of TCP. When they looked closer they found that just a small amount of that individual stave was contaminated. "The extent of this problem is still severely underestimated by coopers and barrel-users," they conclude. Interestingly, barrel-fermented whites are much less affected by TCA-tainted barrels, because the yeasts are very good at adsorbing these haloanisoles in their cell walls. This suggests that if a red barrel is affected, one treatment might be to use inactivated yeast hulls (a common enological additive for improving wine texture and sensory qualities) and stir the barrel once these are added.

Musty taints of wine remain a significant challenge for the wine industry. Natural cork is by far the most significant culprit, but the existence of winery taint and barrel taint means that it is inaccurate and lazy to call all musty taints "cork taint." With the move towards alternative wine closures and the increased quality-control steps by the cork industry, we can expect the incidences of musty taint to fall. But winemakers need to show vigilance in potential sources of musty taints aside from corks, such as wood in the winery or dry goods that have the potential to bring taints into the winery space.

CHAPTER EIGHT

Smoke Taint

- **What is it?** When grapes are exposed to smoke during the ripening process, they can end up making wines that taste ashy, bitter, and unpleasant.
- **What is its flavor impact?** It's not always tasted on the grapes, but it emerges during the winemaking process. Affected wines taste ashy, smoky, and phenolic.
- **What causes it?** Wildfires near vineyards towards the end of the growing season.
- **Is it always bad?** Yes, if it's detectable.
- **How can it be prevented?** There's no way to prevent it, although there are some remedial steps that can take place.
- **How common is it?** Increasingly—in warmer, drier parts of the world—because of the increased incidence of bush/forest fires.

Imagine you're a winegrower in the Yarra Valley. It's February and the growing season has been pretty good so far. Soon it will be vintage time, and you are looking forward to seeing exactly what this year has given you. But wait a minute—what's that on the horizon? A cloud of smoke is approaching; there must be a bushfire nearby. As the smoke cloud gets closer, your heart sinks. Even if the vineyard isn't physically damaged, you know there's a strong chance that this vintage will be ruined by smoke taint. The wine made from these grapes will have a smoky, ashy aftertaste: it's a disaster.

The phenomenon of smoke-tainted wine is emerging as a big problem in many wine regions, with problems encountered in Australia, South Africa, Canada, and California. This is because of the increasing frequency of bushfires in recent years, thought to be a consequence of climate change. As an example, researchers have shown that the increased incidence of forest fires in the western United States—up fourfold since 1986—is due to warmer, drier, and longer summers.[1] In Australia, the bushfire potential is expected to rise by 15–70 percent by 2050.

Wines made from vineyards exposed to smoke can have undesirable smoky or ash-like flavors, but it wasn't until 2003 that this problem was studied with any rigor. In January and February 2003, bushfires in the Australian regions of Victoria and New South Wales resulted in grapes and wines suffering from smoke taint. Consequently, the Industry Services of the AWRI received numerous calls from wineries and growers, prompting them to begin an investigation.[2] They concluded that smoke taint was a real problem, and one of great concern. Many wines from smoke-affected vineyards were indeed displaying characters described in sensory work as "smoky," "burnt," "ash," "ashtray," "salami," and "smoked salmon." They also identified two compounds as key culprits: guaiacol and 4-methylguaiacol. "We were lucky that we already had analytical methods for these two compounds as part of the 'oak suite,'" says Peter

Godden, "and they proved to be a good surrogate for sensory ratings of taint for most juice and wine samples." However, the AWRI researchers commented that there probably were other chemicals involved, albeit at lower concentrations. This study also provided evidence that the taint compounds were found within the skins of the grapes, but not in the pulp or in the surface waxes on the skins.

Smoke-derived flavors, of course, aren't always unpleasant. Deliberate smoke exposure is an important element of the flavor of some cured meats and fish products, and it results in the typical peat and bonfire aromas of Islay whisky. Smoked flavors in some German beers and cheeses come from various smoke-derived volatile compounds such as phenols, carbonyls, lactones, and pyrazines. The most important of these, guaiacol and 4-methylguaiacol, are produced by the action of heat on lignin, a core component of wood. Consequently, in wines that have been aged in oak barrels, which are usually flame or heat toasted before being filled with wine, guaiacol and 4-methylguaiacol are present at concentrations of up to 100 and 20 μg/L, respectively. These concentrations don't seem to be a problem; it's the elevated levels resulting from smoke-exposed grapes that render wines unpalatable, in conjunction with a range of other smoke-taint-related compounds, many of which are currently unidentified.

In this chapter, we'll look at some of the recent research on smoke-tainted wines. When are grapes vulnerable to smoke, and how much smoke exposure constitutes a serious problem? Can winemaking practices have an effect on how much taint occurs in wines made from smoked grapes? Can tainted grapes or wines be treated to remove these unwanted flavors and aromas? And is there a way to test grapes to see whether the wines they produce will be affected by taint?

THE EFFECT OF TIMING AND DURATION OF EXPOSURE

In an important study, Kennison and colleagues (2009)[3] looked at how timing and duration of exposure to smoke affect the level of smoke taint. In the first study of this kind, they applied smoke experimentally to grape vines at various stages of grape development from veraison to harvest. Chemical analysis showed elevated levels of guaiacol, 4-methylguaiacol, 4-ethylguaiacol, and 4-ethylphenol in all the wines made from these vines. In experiments where smoke exposure was repeated, the concentration of these compounds rose in a cumulative fashion. Sensory analysis found aromas of "burnt rubber," "smoked meat," "leather," and "disinfectant" in all wines made from the smoke-exposed vines, but not in control wines. The conclusion was that smoke exposure at any time between veraison and harvest can cause smoke taint, the most sensitive period being a week after veraison and afterward. It is also worth noting that repeated smoke exposure builds up the level of smoke taint, as might be expected. The take-home message: the less smoke the better.

The same authors followed up this work with a more detailed study in 2011[4] in which they looked at the effect of smoke exposure on Merlot vines at twelve different points in the growing season (phenology). The experiment was repeated over three different seasons to check that the effects were consistent year to year. Their results divided the period of active vine growth into three periods of risk from smoke taint. The first, which they termed P1, was from 10 cm shoots to full bloom, and exposure to smoke during this period resulted in low concentrations of volatile phenols in the wine. In P2, which was pea-sized berries to the onset of veraison, moderate and variable levels of taint were seen in the wine. In P3, veraison + 7 days before harvest was the time of peak risk. Average guaiacol and 4-methylguaiacol concentrations in wine were 1.0 and 0.5 mg/L, respectively, for P1; 21.4 and 5.0 mg/L for P2; and 48.9 and 8.9 mg/L for P3. Sensory results were consistent with these chemical analyses.

The authors suggest that the reason the wines in P1 are relatively unaffected is that the berries hadn't yet formed and so had no surface in contact with smoke. It was thought that part of the problem of smoke taint might be the fact that during P3 the berries become a strong sink for photosynthates from the leaves and would likely be taking up taint compounds this way as well as through direct contact with the smoke. But recent studies (at this point still unpublished) indicate that translocation is a tiny factor compared with the direct absorption of smoke compounds onto the developing berries.

The experiment was repeated the following season, and interestingly there was a carryover effect in terms of yields being reduced the year after smoke exposure. Therefore, although there was no carryover effect of taint, this suggests that growers need to leave more buds when they prune a vine that has been affected by smoke, in order to offset the potential yield reduction the following season.

THE EFFECT OF WINEMAKING ON THE EXPRESSION OF SMOKE TAINT

So, if smoke-tainted grapes are coming into the winery, is there a particular way of handling them that will lessen the impact of this taint? In the AWRI study of 2003,[5] guaiacol concentrations in wine were shown to increase with maceration time, and samples macerated with leaves also showed higher levels of guaiacol.

This supported the observation by winemakers that for white wines, machine-harvested fruit was more badly affected than hand-picked fruit, and that free-run juice from whole-bunch pressing was less badly affected than pressings.

The effects of various winemaking approaches on taint levels were studied by Ristic and colleagues (2011).[6] They used grapes that were experimentally smoke affected, as well as grapes harvested from a vineyard in the Yarra Valley that was affected by the bushfires in February and March 2009. A number of different winemaking processes were compared, such as cold maceration (a cold soak to produce a rosé wine), fermentation on skins (to produce a red wine), fermentation with a range of different yeast strains using Grenache grapes, and fermentation with the addition of oak chips or tannins using Shiraz grapes.

The sensory profile of the smoked red wines was dominated by "smoke" and "medicinal" aromas and by "smoky" flavor and "ashy aftertaste." The effect of smoke exposure was more pronounced in the red wines than in the rosé, which suggests that the degree of maceration makes a difference to the smoke-taint character. Eight different yeast strains were tested, and four of these were shown to result in overall lower levels of smoke taint: AWRI 1503, ICV GRE, AWRI Fusion, and SIHA active 3. Interestingly, the intensity of smoke characters was lower in oak- and tannin-treated wines than in controls. This is suspected to be a masking effect, whereby the oak or tannin characters partially hide the smoke taint.

CURING SMOKE TAINT: CAN SMOKE-TAINTED FRUIT OR WINE BE CLEANED?

So, if fruit has been affected by smoke, is there a way of curing this taint, either before or after the wine is made? In the AWRI study of 2003, attempts were made to wash fruit in various ways. The treatments tested were cold water, cold water plus wetting agent, warm water, cold water plus 5 percent ethanol, and milk. None of these worked. This is because the taint compounds are present in the grape skin tissue, not on the surface of the grapes.

One way to reduce or potentially eliminate the presence of smoke-taint compounds from wine is simply to put an adsorptive resin in the wine, a technique called *solid-phase adsorption*. While this will take out the culprit chemicals, it will also remove beneficial flavor and aroma chemicals. An alternative approach is to use reverse osmosis to take out a permeate fraction that contains water, acids, alcohols, and chemicals below a certain molecular point cutoff and then treat this fraction alone, before returning it. Reverse osmosis is commonly used in wineries to remove alcohol from wines: the alcohol is separated from the permeate fraction, and then that fraction minus the alcohol is returned to the wine to create a low-alcohol blending component. For smoke-taint removal, the adsorptive resin treatment is applied just to the permeate, which is then returned to the wine. The hope is that this removes fewer beneficial aroma compounds from the wine than treating the whole wine would.

A trial examining this approach is reported by Fudge and colleagues (2011).[7] Studies were done at both pilot and commercial scales, involving three Pinot Noir wines. Two of these (numbers 1 and 3 in the study) were commercial wines from vineyards that had been affected by smoke taint, whereas the other (number 2) was made from grapes that had been artificially exposed to smoke while they were on the vine. The smoke-derived compounds guaiacol, 4-methylguaiacol, 4-ethylguaiacol, and 4-ethylphenol were tested chemically, and by sensory analysis using panels of trained tasters to compare the difference between treated and untreated wines.

The chemical and sensory data both showed that this treatment is able to remove at least a portion of the smoke-taint compounds: the volatile phenol content of all three wines was decreased significantly. For example, in Pinot Noir 3, guaiacol was reduced from 12 to 3 µg/L and 4-methylguaiacol was reduced from 5 to below 1 µg/L. In the sensory work, the scores for descriptors "smoke aroma," "smoky flavor," and "ashy aftertaste" were all significantly reduced. The treated and untreated wines were also readily differentiated by the tasters (thirty-five, thirty-three, and thirty-three out of forty-eight times for Pinot Noirs 1, 2, and 3, respectively).

A big question is whether the treatment process to remove smoke taint has a negative effect on other wine quality attributes. The study by Fudge and colleagues compared a number of parameters before and after treatment: pH, titratable acidity, sugar and alcohol contents, wine color density, and total phenolics. A small reduction in titratable acidity was observed in the commercial-scale study but not in the pilot scale; this is not considered a big problem. Of the other measures, the only one to change significantly was wine color density. One observation of note is that some of the aroma compounds associated with oak were removed along with the smoke-taint compounds; thus, it is expected that oaked reds will be changed by this process. However, the removal of smoke taint is a big enough incentive to make the loss of a small level of wine quality acceptable.

BOUND AND FREE FORMS OF THE
SMOKE-TAINT COMPOUNDS

One interesting observation by Fudge and colleagues was that in some cases, smoke taint can return in clean, treated wines after storage in barrel or after a period in bottle. A gradual increase in guaiacol and 4-methylguaiacol was noted in both treated and untreated wines. They explained this by noting that a portion of these compounds are transformed in the plant tissue to chemically altered or bound forms (in this case they were *glycoconjugated,* a term that refers to molecules reacting chemically with carbohydrates such as sugars) and that after bottle aging, the glycoconjugated forms revert back to the original compounds by the process of hydrolysis. The reverse osmosis process removes only the compounds themselves and not their glycoconjugates, which means that it is inadvisable to cellar wines that have been treated for smoke taint in this way. This theory was demonstrated in a paper by Singh and colleagues (2011),[8] who studied grapes and wines affected by bushfires in the King Valley, Victoria, in 2006 and 2007. They showed that bound volatiles act as reserve for guaiacol, 4-methylguaiacol, and other compounds, which are released during the aging of wines, with the bound forms acting as a reservoir for the taint compounds.

A paper by Wilkinson and colleagues (2011)[9] also addressed this issue. They were looking at analytical techniques that winemakers could employ to see whether their grapes were damaged by smoke or not, and thus answer the important question of whether they were going to produce tainted wine. This would be very important for winemakers buying grapes from regions where just some of the vineyards might have been affected by bushfires. The problem is that measuring for the taint compounds themselves isn't reliable enough: the levels of guaiacol and 4-methylguaiacol in grapes don't always correlate with the extent of taint in wines made from them. Wilkinson and colleagues used a range of analytical methods to measure the concentration of smoke-related phenols and their conjugated (bound) forms in affected grapes and wines and found a strong correlation between the levels of glycoconjugated phenols and the level of taint. This is because winemaking releases guaiacol and 4-methylguaiacol from their conjugated form through hydrolysis reactions that occur in the acidic environment of juice and wine. The conclusion is that it would be worth analyzing grapes for the glycoconjugated forms of these smoke-related phenols,[10] because their presence at significant levels could avoid the expense of harvesting and processing badly tainted grapes that would make wines of an unacceptable commercial standard.

This also means that it's not always possible for winemakers to taste smoke taint in affected grapes. The grape vine sticks sugars on the smoke-taint compounds (forming glycoconjugates), and these need to be removed (cleaved) by enzymes called *glycosidases*. We have these enzymes in our saliva, so after a while in the mouth we might smell and taste the taint compounds, but people differ in their glycosidase levels in saliva. So, if you want to test grapes for the effects of smoke taint, you need to get some yeast action, cleaving the sugars off the taint compounds, and then do sensory testing.

At the AWRI, the current model for smoke taint is one part guaiacol and 1.5 parts each of the three cresols in a neutral wine that is known not to contain those compounds. But they acknowledge that the impact of smoke taint can be quite different each season: it's not a fixed taint in terms of the chemicals or the sensory impact they have.

Smoke taint is a big issue in regions subject to forest fires, and this is an important subject. But it's difficult to see what can be done once grapes have been affected by smoke: some quality loss is pretty much inevitable, even if remedial steps are taken.

TABLE 4

Chemicals Associated with Smoke Taint in Wine

Compound	Notes
Guaiacol	The main smoke-taint compound, with aromas of smoke, phenols, and leather. Detectable in wine at levels of around 25 μg/L, and can reach concentrations of 1,500 μg/L in wine made from grapes that see repeated smoke exposure. Also present in oaked wines at lower levels.
4-Methylguaiacol	The second most important smoke-taint compound, with aromas of toast and ash. Detectable in wine at levels of 65 μg/L, and can be present at levels of 300 μg/L in smoke-tainted wines. Also present in oaked wines.
4-Ethylphenol	This volatile phenol is one of the main compounds responsible for the sensory impact of *Brettanomyces*. Has phenolic, horsey, and animal-like aromas. Detectable in wine at levels around 600 μg/L, but present at lower levels in smoke-tainted wines.
4-Ethylguaiacol	Also one of the main compounds in *Brettanomyces* aroma. Described as having smoky, spicy, toasted, and bread aromas. Detectable in wine at levels of around 100 μg/L, and present at around this level in smoke-tainted wines.
Eugenol	Spicy, clove-like aroma. Has been found at 20 μg/L in smoke-tainted wine, but absent from controls. Present in oak-aged wines.
Furfural	Sweet butterscotch, caramel, and toast aromas. Has been found at 15 μg/L in smoke-tainted wine, but absent from controls. Present in oak-aged wines.
Cresols	The *p*-, *m*-, and *o*-cresols are important contributors to smoke taint. These are methylphenols with a distinctive coal-tar smell.

OTHER ENVIRONMENTAL TAINTS

In 2007, celebrated viticulturist Dr. Richard Smart was asked to compile an independent report on the possible impact of a proposed pulp mill in the Tamar Valley of Tasmania, which was to be built by the owners of the Tamar Ridge winery, the Gunns, who employed Smart as viticultural advisor from 2003 on. Smart concluded that there would be no negative effect of the pulp mill on neighboring vineyards. Adrian Coulter of the AWRI disagreed and wrote a letter in response, outlining historical cases where factory emissions have ended up affecting vineyards and tainting wines. "Grapevine leaves have a huge surface area," says Coulter, "and the skins [also] have a huge surface area that's a great solvent for things like that." In 1973, two Swiss researchers, Tanner and Sandoz, published a study in which they linked phenolic taints in wines in central Switzerland to the proximity of vineyards to a copper-wire-insulating factory. They found cresols (phenolic compounds) in the air and also in tainted wines. The same authors also found tainted wines near a railway-sleeper processing factory and a bitumen factory. In 1977, De Pe and colleagues looked at tainted wines in the northern Italian region of Valtellina and found phenolic taints near a chemical plant. If a factory is releasing anything into the air, there is the danger of contaminating nearby vineyards and hence wines.

Some terms commonly used to describe smoke-taint characters in wine:

- Ash/ash tray
- Burning
- Burnt rubber

- Smoky
- Smoked meat/smoked sausage/salami
- Leather
- Phenolic
- Disinfectant/hospitals
- Musty
- Caramel

CHAPTER NINE

Geosmin

- **What is it?** An earthy-smelling sesquiterpene produced by *Penicillium expansum*. It's a microbial fault that seems to be common in damper vintages. It's also encountered as a cork taint.
- **What is its flavor impact?** It causes both red and white wines to smell of freshly turned earth, beetroot, and mustiness.
- **What causes it?** It's caused by the growth of *P. expansum* on grape bunches that have already been attacked by *Botrytis cinerea,* and by mold growth on cork during processing.
- **Is it always bad?** Yes, if it's detectable.
- **How can it be prevented?** It's very hard to spot, unfortunately. Extra vigilance is needed during harvest to make sure that contaminated bunches don't get into the vat.
- **How common is it?** It depends on the vintage and location. It seems to be more common in damper

vintages in cooler climates. I'm not aware of data on its incidence. It's a taint that is relatively new to many tasters, and it can be confused with cork taint.

In 2012, I was judging Sauvignon Blancs from the Loire Valley, most of which were from the 2011 vintage. Time after time, I encountered wines that had a faint hint of what's best described as freshly turned earth, beetroot, and old cellars. It wasn't cork taint: it was almost certainly geosmin (I can't be sure, of course, because we didn't do any chemical analysis). Those of us who were tasting got to know it quite well by the end of the week.

Darriet and colleagues[1] first identified geosmin as a wine fault in 2000. They studied a set of red and white wines of different origins, described as smelling of freshly tilled earth and damp cellars. They analyzed these wines by gas chromatography–olfactometry, finding the relevant compound that contributes this aroma; then they used gas chromatography–mass spectrometry to identify it chemically as geosmin (trans-1,10-dimethyl-trans-9-decalol), which is a sesquiterpene. They found that it was present in juice taken from freshly crushed grapes, indicating that microbes that had developed on the grapes were responsible.

One of Darriet's students, Stéphane La Guerche, then carried out a study to identify the cause of geosmin in grapes, which ran over four seasons from 1999 to 2002. The results were published in 2005.[2] La Guerche looked at the microbial populations in rotten grapes with geosmin contamination over four different regions in France. In particular, he looked at two species of microbes known to be capable of producing geosmin: a filamentous bacterium, *Streptomyces,* and a fungus, *Penicillium.* The interesting finding was that grapes with geosmin taint also had *Botrytis cinerea* present, even though this couldn't produce geosmin.

The conclusion of the study was that *Penicillium expansum* was the main culprit, but on its own it can't produce geosmin in grapes: it needs to have the complementary action of *Botrytis* on the grapes in order to do this.

Geosmin is a problem because it is quite a potent contaminant. The odor threshold for geosmin is 0.0082–0.018 ppb (in water), which is very low. So you don't need too many affected bunches in the must in order to have an issue.

How can it be cured? There are several options, which were recently evaluated in a study by Lisanti and colleagues[3] from Naples, Italy. They compared seven techniques for removing geosmin from wine:

· activated charcoal
· bentonite
· PVPP
· yeast cell walls
· potassium caseinate
· zeolite
· grape seed oil

These are added to wine to adsorb the geosmin, in a sort of fining action. They are nonspecific, so the big question is, if they take out the geosmin, what else do they remove, and is this compromise worth making? In red wine, they found that potassium caseinate decreased geosmin by 14 percent and grape seed oil reduced it by 83 percent. In white wine, activated charcoal reduced it by 23 percent and grape seed oil by 81 percent. But these treatments also reduced desirable volatile compounds, and in particular the fruity-smelling esters. The best overall treatment turned out to be grape seed oil, which reduced the geosmin more than it did the desirable aromas.

One study suggests that geosmin may be more of a problem than is realized. A 2010 paper by Weingart and colleagues[4] from the University of Vienna looked at 117 Austrian wines: eighty-nine whites (sixty-three of which had been flagged as potentially faulty by sensory analysis) and twenty-eight reds (sixteen flagged as potentially faulty), carrying out chemical analysis for geosmin and 2,4,6-trichloroanisole (TCA; the main cork-taint compound). The results were surprising: 93 percent of all the wines had geosmin above the limit of detection (0.5 ng/L), and 55 percent of them had it at levels over 2 ng/L. The highest level of geosmin found was 16.7 ng/L. While TCA was found in 24 percent of the wines, it was in only five wines (4 percent of the total) that were classified during sensory analysis as "corky" or "corky and moldy." The researchers suggested that chemical analysis is needed to verify claims of cork taint. At lower levels of taint, professionals might be confusing geosmin and cork taint, with the former being more prevalent than people had realized.

So, geosmin is a fault that we all need to be aware of. In particular, vigilance during rain-affected harvests is needed, because it may be that affected bunches aren't immediately apparent. This is one of those faults that, once you've recognized it, you get better at spotting. It's also another fault where people seem to differ quite a bit in their sensitivity, at least from my experience.

CHAPTER TEN

Eucalyptus Taint

- **What is it?** When grapes are grown in proximity to eucalyptus trees, the resulting wines can develop a eucalypt character.
- **What is its flavor impact?** Affected wines are described as minty, medicinal, and eucalypt-like.
- **What causes it?** An aromatic compound called *cineole*, from the leaves of the trees, finds its way onto grape skins, and from there into the wine. It's also transmitted by tainted leaf and bark material that finds its way into the wine, which may be the most significant cause of the problem.
- **Is it always bad?** No: some people like it. In some red wines it can enhance fruitiness at low levels.
- **How can it be prevented?** By not planting eucalypt plantations near vineyards, and by the use of management strategies, such as minimizing material other than grapes in picking bins, or picking the few rows closest to

the trees separately, and then back blending the wine carefully.

- **How common is it?** In Australia it's very common indeed because of the prevalence of eucalypts. It's far more common in reds than in whites because of the skin maceration.

Eucalyptus is such a distinctive smell for me. As a child, I remember holidays camping in the south of Spain on a site with eucalyptus trees providing much-needed shade. In the intense heat of the middle of the day, the oils from the leaves vaporized and filled the air. To this day, that smell brings back powerful memories.

When vineyards are planted close to eucalyptus trees, the trees can have a direct influence on the flavor of the wine, and this can be a problem.[1] Sometimes, it reaches levels where it can be called a fault. The leaves of eucalypts have oil glands that secrete 1,8-cineole (known as "eucalyptol"), which is responsible for the distinctive eucalyptus smell, and this can end up in the wine.

One study from the AWRI examined this. They looked at wines made from grapes at different proximities to eucalyptus trees in the Yarra Valley. Wines from vines within 50 m of trees had levels of cineole of 15.5 µg/L, while those farther away had just 0.1 µg/L. In another study of a vineyard in Western Australia, wine made from rows that were 11.0–18.5 m from the eucalypts (blue gums) had 9.5 µg/L of cineole, while those 50 m away had 1.6 µg/L, and those 230 m away had levels of 0.4 µg/L. The fact that just red wines show this character suggests that it is simply a matter of the oils collecting on the skins; red wines are made with extended skin contact, whereas white grapes are usually pressed straightaway. In red wines, the eucalypt character tends to come across as a minty, slightly medicinal smell and flavor. In sensory studies, the impact has been described as "eucalyptus," "fresh," "cool," "medicinal," and "camphoraceous." Interestingly, while white wines usually don't have this minty character, "orange wines" (white wines made with extended skin contact) can demonstrate some of these minty, medicinal characters.

As well as the cineole collecting on the skins of the grapes, there is also the possibility that eucalyptus leaves could be getting into fermenting vats when grapes are machine picked. The evidence for this is that less eucalyptol is found in wine made from hand-picked grapes. However, it's possible that even in hand-picked fruit, eucalyptus leaves could be hiding in bunches and end up in the wine this way.

Cineole represents 65–75 percent of the oil secreted from the leaves of eucalyptus trees. So how much of this is needed for us to be able to detect it? ETS Laboratories in California studied the aroma thresholds for eucalyptol using a California Merlot. The difference threshold (where people can notice something different about the wine) and the recognition threshold (where people can specify what's different about it) were 1.1 μg/L and 3.2 μg/L, respectively. Australian studies show a threshold of 2.2–3.2 μg/L, and a consumer rejection threshold of 27 μg/L. Anecdotal reports from the AWRI's Advanced Wine Assessment Courses demonstrate a very large spread of sensitivities to this compound. "The sensitive people dotted around the room consistently call the same wines for elevated eucalyptus," reports the AWRI's Peter Godden, "when others don't see what they are talking about."

ETS also did an experiment in which Cabernet Sauvignon berries were placed into a sealed jar containing one eucalyptus leaf for five days, making sure that the leaf was not in direct contact with the berries. Eucalyptol was detectable in the berries after this short period, but not in control jars where there were no leaves.

Some people like the eucalypt character in red wine. After all, it's relatively common in Australian reds. In South Africa, Stellenbosch producer Thelema has actually released a "Mint" Cabernet Sauvignon, which is a premium wine with a distinctive eucalypt character made from portions of the vineyard nearest eucalyptus trees. It's odd but quite nice. So this is one of those faults that is context and subject dependent.

One Australian study attempted to determine the consumer rejection threshold for eucalypt character in red wines by spiking the same wine with different levels of cineole. They came up with a figure of 27.5 µg/L and concluded that a moderate intensity of eucalypt character in red wine should not be considered a taint, and that some consumers may consider moderate intensities preferable to no eucalypt character. In another Australian study by the sensory team at the AWRI, they found that consumers preferred red wine (a bag-in-box Merlot) spiked with cineole (at 4 and 30 µg/L) over unspiked wine, with a cluster (38 percent) preferring the wine spiked at the higher level.[2] "People see eucalyptus as a taint," says Adrian Coulter of the AWRI, "but from my experiences during tastings where we spike wines with it, people like it. And there's a handful of people who like it at huge concentrations." He adds, "It can increase the fruitiness. When I spike cheaper wines with cineole, to me they are massively improved."

Another Australian study, also by the AWRI, surveyed 146 commercially available red wines made from a range of varieties; 40 percent contained eucalyptol above the reported aroma detection threshold of 1.1 µg/L, and several contained relatively high amounts (5–20 µg/L). The highest level of eucalyptol found was 19.6 µg/L, and this was made from a vineyard that had eucalyptus trees close by. They also looked at forty-four white wines, and the highest level of eucalyptol found in those was

0.8 µg/L, which would be expected, because this character, if present, is only extracted during maceration of skins.

In some ways, you could consider eucalypt character in wines to be a direct terroir effect. It is commonly thought that this character comes from the cineole-containing oil from the leaves finding its way onto grapes and then persists through fermentation to the final wine. It follows that any winegrower who doesn't desire this character in their wine should selectively harvest any vines in the proximity of eucalyptus trees and not allow this fruit into their fermentations. It would be interesting to see whether there are similar effects with oil-producing plants other than eucalyptus. For example, is the *garrigue* character that is so often present in wines from the south of France a direct result of oils from the aromatic plants common in the region?

Eucalypt character is potentially beneficial in some wines. At low levels it has been shown to enhance fruitiness in Australian Cabernet Sauvignons, and it has been proposed as a marker to identify Australian red wines.[3] Related to this, there's a possibility that pine trees might be having a similar effect to eucalypts. There's no evidence supporting this statement, but when you walk close to pines on a hot day they are powerfully aromatic. One winemaker I know is convinced that some Bordeaux wines have a slightly pine-like character when the vineyards have pine trees in close proximity.

CONFIRMING THE SOURCE OF CINEOLE IN WINES

Dimitra Capone and her colleagues at the AWRI have done quite a bit of work looking to confirm the airborne-transmission hypothesis of eucalypt character in wine. Is it the oil in the air, getting on the grapes, that is primarily responsible? They took a vineyard next to a stand of eucalyptus trees and looked at the concentration of cineole in grapes, leaves, and stems of vines in row 1 (right next to the trees), row 10, row 20, and row 60 (farthest away). Interestingly, they found the highest levels in leaves, then stems, and then much lower levels in grapes. The levels of cineole decreased with distance from the trees.

They also used traps to see whether cineole was coming from the atmosphere. These consisted of polyethylene sheets that were held between wire mesh and then placed in both horizontal and vertical orientations in rows 1, 10, 20, and 60. The levels of cineole found on the traps correlated with the grape, leaf, and stem data to a degree, but there wasn't enough to account for the total amount of cineole in the wines.

Capone and colleagues also came up with results showing that the presence of eucalyptus leaves or pieces of bark in the canopies of the vine could be a significant contributor to eucalyptol in wine. Eucalypts shed their bark and leaves at regular intervals, and these can blow in the wind quite a distance from the trees. They found them lodged in the canopies of vines and enclosed in bunches. Capone thinks that they are of greater importance to the ultimate 1,8-cineole concentrations in the wine than airborne transmission of volatiles. They found thirty-three eucalyptus leaves in 550 kg of hand-picked fruit. The levels in machine-picked fruit would likely be higher. It is now accepted that eucalyptus leaves and bark are a significant contributor to this character in affected wines.

AVOIDING EUCALYPT CHARACTER IN WINE

What are the steps to avoid eucalypt character in wine? When there are eucalypts near a vineyard, it makes sense to harvest the rows closest to the trees by hand and process the fruit separately. It is possible to blend this back in later on, should some level of eucalypt character be desirable. Low levels seem to have good consumer acceptance. To minimize the character, the fact that it isn't just airborne oil transmission that is significant offers up some management practices that could have an effect. The first is to pick potentially affected rows by hand, taking care not to include any eucalyptus leaf or bark in the fermentation. After picking, by machine or hand, a sorting table can be used to remove any of these leaves, or any vine leaves, which have much higher levels than grapes.

Eucalypt character is a very interesting fault or taint because, once again, it can have a positive effect in certain wines at certain levels. It is much more desirable in Cabernet Sauvignon, for example, than in Pinot Noir. Peter Godden says that when wines are spiked with cineole, he sees the red fruit character coming out very strongly. "In one of the vineyards that we looked at eucalyptus in, in South Australia, we believe that the company blends these wines up to a certain level of cineole," he says, "which they like, and which the consumers like." It really is a curious taint.

CHAPTER ELEVEN

Light Damage

- **What is it?** Loss of quality caused by exposing wine to light.
- **What is its flavor impact?** It causes oxidation of the wine by depleting free SO_2 levels and/or causes the development of off-odors from volatile sulfur compounds.
- **What causes it?** Two mechanisms: either the formation of glyoxylic acid from tartaric acid in the presence of iron or photogeneration of volatile sulfur compounds from methionine and cysteine.
- **Is it always bad?** Yes, if it's detectable.
- **How can it be prevented?** By bottling in colored glass and/or keeping wine away from light.
- **How common is it?** More common in rosés, which are almost always bottled in clear glass, and more common in sparkling wines. Not a rare fault.

In this chapter and the next, we'll look at two wine faults that take place after bottling: loss of quality that comes from exposure to excessive temperatures and inappropriate exposure to light. We'll start with light.

There are two distinct mechanisms through which light damages wine. The first involves transition metal ions and tartaric acid. When iron is present in wine, it can form a complex with tartaric acid, and this complex is capable of absorbing light, which breaks up the tartaric acid to form glyoxylic acid. Iron is typically present in wine at concentrations of 2–20 mg/L, with an average level of around 5. The Fe^{3+} ion forms a complex with tartaric acid that can act as a photochemical agent, and the result is glyoxylic acid.[1] This is bad news: it binds with SO_2 and can rapidly deplete free SO_2. In a typical white wine with 5 g/L tartaric acid, a conversion of just 1.5 percent of the tartaric acid to glyoxylic acid is needed to deplete 30 mg/L of free SO_2, which is all the average white wine would have in the first place. If SO_2 is absent or depleted, then the glyoxylic acid can react with the skin phenolics to form a yellow colored xanthylium pigment, which can cause browning of the wine.

The wavelengths most effective in producing glyoxylic acid are 300–520 nm, which spans near UV and visible blue light. So this is where the color of the wine bottle comes in. These days, there are commercial incentives to bottle rosé and some white wines in clear glass, but this isn't good for quality. All glass bottles cut out light below 300 nm in wavelength. But for cutting out other wavelengths, the best color is amber, then antique green; clear glass is the worst by far. Of the colored bottles, heavier ones transmit less light than lighter ones.

A second sort of light damage is what is known more commonly as *light strike*. It was first identified in 1983 by Maujean and Seguin as *gout de lumière,* and it involves the formation of volatile sulfur compounds derived from methionine and cysteine. In this process, vitamin B2 (riboflavin) undergoes photoactivation and reduction with light in the 370–440 nm range. This leads to the photogeneration of the volatile sulfur compounds such as mercaptans (thiols) and dimethyl sulfide. The descriptors commonly used for this light strike are "skunky," "cooked cabbage," and "onion/garlic." It seems that the main risk factor for wines that are going to see some light is the concentration of riboflavin. Traditional-method sparkling wines are more at risk than still wines, it is thought, because of the liberation of amino acids (including the two baddies, cysteine and methionine) from yeast cells during the autolysis process that takes place in the *tirage* stage. Bentonite fining reduces riboflavin levels, so where this occurs it may lessen the risk.

Clearly, this is a fault that is avoidable. The first step would be to use colored glass bottles that don't allow the damaging wavelengths of light through. If this is not possible from a commercial viewpoint (it is pretty much impossible to sell rosé wines in colored glass these days, although the British retailer Marks and Spencer bravely held out for a while for quality reasons), then care must be taken not to expose bottles to light.

CHAPTER TWELVE

Heat Damage

- **What is it?** High temperatures affecting wine chemistry in negative ways.
- **What is its flavor impact?** Wines age prematurely and are prone to oxidation.
- **What causes it?** The high temperatures accelerate aging and may also cause reactions to take place in the wine that would be unlikely at lower temperatures.
- **Is it always bad?** Yes, if it's detectable.
- **How can it be prevented?** By being careful with logistics: shipping wine in refrigerated containers, making sure that road transit doesn't take place at the hottest time of year, and not leaving pallets of wine lying around in the sun.
- **How common is it?** Studies suggest that quite a bit of wine quality is routinely lost through heat exposure in the logistics chain.

What about heat damage? This is potentially a huge problem, because wine is at risk of being exposed to high temperatures while in the logistics chain. Wine is commonly shipped through the hot equatorial regions, and if it is transported in normal, unrefrigerated containers it can see high temperatures, especially if it's stuck in the docks somewhere like Singapore. You can pay for refrigerated containers, but this is quite expensive and not always available. Alternatively, you can specify below-deck storage to protect the containers from the risk of being exposed to direct sunlight, but remember that the fuel oil for these container ships needs to be heated before it is used and so there's still a risk of high temperatures below the deck, depending on where the container ends up. Then, too, ground shipping can be risky at certain times of year.

A few years ago, I was visiting a friend who imports natural wines into Singapore. He sat me down and gave me three glasses of wine blind. I tasted, and the wines seemed to be all the same. But when I really focused, one was slightly different. The difference wasn't marked, but it was there. He told me that it was indeed the same wine, but the one that was different had been shipped from France in an unrefrigerated container by mistake. He ended up having to battle with the shipping company to get the cost of the wine refunded, because he couldn't sell the wine to his customers in good faith if it had been affected by the shipping process. He eventually won, and he sold the wine at a reduced price, explaining with a label why it was being sold more cheaply. This wine wasn't completely ruined, but it was different: some quality had been lost.

There have been a few studies of the effect of elevated temperatures, and the picture that emerges is of high temperatures, more than fluctuations in temperature, causing the damage. For example, Marais looked at the effects of twelve months' storage at 30°C and showed that it results in decreased quality and faulty flavors.[1] In a paper published in 1985, Ough found that just a few days at 40°C can result in visual and sensory changes.[2]

In 1996, a team of French researchers at Inter Rhône Technical Services looked at the effects of four different storage conditions—designed to simulate conditions in a cellar, on display shelves, and during shipping—on four reds and one rosé wine.[3] Bottles were sampled at regular intervals over a two-year period by chemical and sensory analysis. The wines that were kept at a constant low temperature (14°C) with the bottle lying down performed much better than the other three.

In 2010, a more detailed study took place in collaboration between the University of California, Davis, and Murdoch University in Western Australia.[4] Four white wines and four reds were exposed to four conditions: 20°C, 40°C, alternating 20°C and 40°C, and putting some of the wines into the trunk of a car for three weeks! After this abuse, the thirty-two treatments (i.e., eight wines in each of the four conditions) were evaluated using sensory and chemical analysis. The results showed that the wines stored at higher temperatures had been significantly affected, with loss of fruit characters and more flavors associated with old wines, which were totally out of place in such young bottles.

In 2001, the American Vineyard Foundation issued a report, authored by Christian Butzke of the University of California, Davis, which monitored heat exposure during wine shipments within the United States. This was in collaboration with Robert Mondavi Family of Wineries and Delicato Vineyards. They prepared packages consisting of a sealed standard wine bottle filled with a wine-like alcohol/water mix containing a temperature sensor in the center of the liquid, attached to an external data logger that recorded a temperature every fifteen minutes. The packages accompanied twenty or so commercial cross-country shipments with multiple packages in different positions within the container. The conclusions were that wines experienced lots of variation in temperature, but that this depended to a degree on where they were located in the container. There were potentially damaging highs, and potentially damaging rapid fluctuations. When applying a general rule of thumb for the increase in the rate of chemical reactions with temperature rises, they calculated that the wines were exposed to heat that represented an aging time equivalent to between one month and six years.

In 2002, Meyer published a literature review[5] on the impact of shipping temperatures on wine that cited numerous published and unpublished studies and came up with some interesting points. For example, in 2000, the Ontario Liquor Control Board brought in 21,500 containers of wines and spirits, just 22 percent of which were in temperature-controlled containers. Studies in South Africa showed that one of the most vulnerable points in the logistics chain was in the harbor, where temperatures ranged from 45°C to −10°C. This resulted in large peaks inside the containers. Meyer noted a potential ameliorating factor: reusable insulation quilts. When U.S. winery Turner Road tested the effectiveness of space blankets (essentially bubble wrap with a metallic layer), they found that under an ambient temperature of 38°C, the wine under the blanket peaked below 29°C, a potentially significant difference. At the time, the cost of this blanket was $135, and the return cost around $25, depending on where it was sent from. Assuming five uses, this resulted in a cost of five cents per case. One U.S. study showed that when a wine was shipped from California to Atlanta, it peaked at 43°C, but with the insulating blanket it was 32–35°C. In a shipment traveling from South Africa to Japan, the temperature outside the liner peaked at 41°C, while inside it was 33°C.

A 2012 study tracked international wine shipments to the United States from Australia, collecting temperature data for wine shipments.[6] The individual trip legs were analyzed, looking at thresholds in temperature levels and fluctuations. Bottled wines are subject to wide variations in temperature during shipping. In this study, 154 data loggers were used to collect readings at two-hour intervals for the entire journey from winery to destination; data were recovered from fifty-seven of the loggers. The data indicate that there are three distinct stages of transport: first the container is transported within Australia, from winery to port of origin; then it travels by sea to the U.S. port; and finally it is transported by land from the U.S. port to the importer's location. The sea leg of the journey showed fairly consistent temperatures, but the two land legs seemed to show worrying extremes and lots of variation. Only two of the loggers picked up temperatures over 40°C, which is encouraging. But one logger showed that its shipment spent ten hours over 40°C, with a maximum temperature of 50°C. That shipment spent 250 hours over 25°C, which is extremely concerning. Among the data from all fifty-seven loggers, the proportion of hours spent at 25°C and above was highest for the U.S. leg (22 percent), followed by the sea leg (13 percent), and then the Australian leg (1 percent).

The temperature inside a shipping container can get very high. If the outside temperature is 40°C, the inside of an uninsulated container can be as high as 60°C. Temperature can also affect wine in cold conditions: although wine won't freeze until it reaches −5°C, at 0°C it will often throw deposits of tartrate crystals. Wine can be protected by using refrigerated containers (reefers) or, more affordably, special thermal blankets or reflective container liners. This adds expense, though, and the wine industry can't always afford these measures.

In 2014, Du Toit and Piquet used simulated shipping conditions to look at their effects on wine quality, using a Chenin Blanc and a Sauvignon Blanc as the test wines.[7] The wines were stored at variable temperatures over a period of forty-six days to simulate a typical export journey from dockyard (in South African) to Europe; they were also stored at a range of constant temperatures (−4°C, 15°C, and 37°C). The clearest effect on wine quality was seen with the constant 37°C treatment. The other three treatments showed no significant differences for the Chenin Blanc; for the Sauvignon Blanc, there was a small but significant difference with the constant −4°C treatment, which was preferred. This is likely because the fruity polyfunctional thiol 3-MHA is preserved better by this storage temperature—it is lost fairly quickly by acid hydrolysis at higher temperatures. The authors concluded that it is high average temperature that is damaging to wine quality, rather than fluctuations.

Increasingly, wines are being shipped in bulk and then bottled in the destination country. There are two methods for bulk shipment. The first uses ISO tanks—reusable stainless steel tanks with a 26,000 L capacity—designed to fit on trucks and for easy transport by sea, rail, or road. These are good for wine because they don't allow oxygen ingress, but they carry all sorts of liquids and need to be cleaned thoroughly between uses. The second method, which is increasingly popular, uses flexitanks. These are single-use bags that are placed inside standard 20-foot (6.25 m) shipping containers and then filled with 24,000 L of wine (although smaller versions also exist). The latest generation of flexitanks are much better at keeping oxygen out than the earlier versions and are made of polyethylene, with an ethylene vinyl alcohol (EVOH) copolymer that acts as a barrier material. But oxygen pickup during transport, and also during loading and unloading of the tank at either end, is still a concern. The big advantage of bulk shipping is the thermal inertia of a large body of wine like this. It protects against thermal spikes along the logistics chain, and all the wine is the same (with bottled wine, there will be some variability depending on where the bottle is positioned in the shipment). An unpublished internal study from Trans Ocean Distribution (part of the Hillebrand group of logistics companies) has monitored the effects of temperature on wine transported in bulk in flexitanks, as cited in a publication by the British organization WRAP.[8] These studies show that the large thermal mass, coupled with the convective mixing currents, effectively dampens out all large temperature spikes. Instead, the wine experiences a more gentle temperature swing during transport, without the potentially damaging highs.

As far as I am aware, no one has compared wines sealed with different closures to see whether they are affected differently by changes in temperature. There's a possibility that wines sealed with in-neck closures, such as corks and synthetic corks, could be affected more by fluctuations in temperature than those with screw caps. Potentially, this could be because of piston-like behavior with changes in temperature, creating a pressure differential between the ullage space and the air outside the bottle. This might lead to extra air entering the bottle, increasing the oxygen exposure of the wine. Also, the oxygen transmission properties of materials change with temperature—another possible factor. It would be interesting to research this question. With standard ullage, corks get pushed out when wine temperature is between

32°C and 38°C. A pushed-out cork renders a wine unsalable, but at least it's proof that the wine will have experienced damaging temperatures: with screw caps, this undesirable history of the wine remains a secret.

While heat damage doesn't fall into the standard category of faults or taints, it is certainly a way that wine quality can be lost, and it's also pretty much hidden. It's a subject that the trade doesn't discuss very much, but in the real world, if wine is shipped long distances via very warm places, there's a high risk that it may have experienced temperatures that will have caused some loss of quality. Wineries and wine retail buyers alike should be extremely concerned about this issue and exercise diligence in mitigating this risk all the way through the logistics chain.

CHAPTER THIRTEEN

Greenness in Wine and Ladybug Taint

- **What is it?** Excessive green flavors in wine are caused by unripe grapes, but they can also be the result of ladybugs in the grape clusters.
- **What is its flavor impact?** Green flavors, such as cut grass and green pepper. When ladybugs are involved, affected wines are described as having flavors of greenness, peanuts, and earth.
- **What causes it?** A group of compounds called methoxypyrazines, which humans are very sensitive to, but also other molecules such as green leafy aldehydes.
- **Is it always bad?** Some wines can cope better with greenness than others. But ladybug taint is always bad because it is so extreme.
- **How can it be prevented?** By picking grapes riper, by changing the light environment of the grape cluster, or, in the case of ladybug taint, by trying not to let the beetles get into the must. There are also remedial

actions under development for treating excessively green wines.

·   **How common is it?** Mild greenness is very common, and not undesirable. Excessive greenness and ladybug taint are quite rare and depend on the season.

A while back, there was an interesting controversy about red wines from the 2004 vintage in Burgundy. They tasted odd. Burgundy lover Bill Nanson, who runs the website Burgundy-Report.com, was the first to raise the issue, suggesting that it might be caused by ladybugs (or ladybirds, their English name outside of North America). He noted that around 30 percent of cuvées had a strange aromatic profile, and he linked it to his experience of grape-baskets during harvest time in 2004 often having dozens of ladybugs in them. His theory was that the off-putting green notes characteristic of many of the wines of this vintage were caused by methoxypyrazines, released by ladybugs present on the grape clusters, that had found their way into the fermenting vat.

In fact, while this was new to Burgundy, the wine world's attention was first brought to the issue of ladybug taint a few years earlier. In the 2001 vintage in Canada's Niagara region, the infestation was so large that more than a million liters of wine had to be dumped. The culprit was identified as the multi-colored Asian lady beetle *(Harmonia axyridis)*,[1] which had been introduced to Canada and the United States back in 1916 as a biological control agent. It was brought into France in 1982, but its spread through Europe has been relatively recent; it has only really dispersed widely since 2002.

The ladybugs tend to aggregate on grape clusters near harvest, and subsequently they may end up in the fermentation vat. They are found feeding on the sugar in grapes, but it seems that they are able to feed only on damaged grapes. When they are crushed during fermentation, they release their hemolymph, which contains high levels of an extremely potent methoxypyrazine, isopropyl methoxypyrazine (IPMP). (The main methoxypyrazine present in some grapes, which causes the distinctive green pepper character, is the related isobutyl methoxypyrazine, or IBMP.)

Wines affected with ladybug taint are described as showing "peanut," "green (bell) pepper," "asparagus," and "earthy/herbaceous" aromas. Methoxypyrazines are highly potent aroma compounds, and we are able to detect them at very low levels. The bad news: unlike many other aromas in wine, they don't diminish with time in bottle.

METHOXYPYRAZINES: KEY SOURCE OF GREENNESS

In addition to the two already mentioned, there's a third methoxypyrazine that has been found in grapes and wine, 3-sec-butyl-methoxypyrazine. All are responsible for the distinctive "greenness." There's a level at which these green flavors can be typical of certain varieties—the Cabernet family seems to show them as a varietal characteristic, and they work well in Sauvignon Blanc—but they are unpleasant when they are too high. Viticulturists work hard with red varieties to diminish methoxypyrazines by using techniques to increase bunch light exposure. This is a delicate balancing act, because while light exposure reduces methoxypyrazine levels, it can also result in sunburned grapes. A good compromise is to manage the canopy so as to allow dappled light to penetrate, or to manage it so that the east-facing side of the canopy, which has less of the damaging afternoon sun, has more fruit-zone leaf removal than the west. In cooler climates, the entire fruit zone is often denuded of leaves.

Humans are incredibly sensitive to methoxypyrazines and can pick them up at very low concentrations: the detection thresholds are 2.1 ng/L for IBMP and just 320 pg/L for IPMP (pg = picograms), but there's variation according to which wine context they are found in. There are also interindividual differences in their detection: some people can pick up IPMP at 320 pg/L while others only spot it at 95 ng/L, which is roughly a 300-fold difference. They survive fermentation pretty much intact and don't change much in bottle over time.

There are two sources of methoxypyrazines in wine. The first is grapes: levels are high in unripe grapes and then diminish with ripening, so in cool climates where grapes struggle to ripen they can be elevated. But perhaps more worrying is the contribution made by ladybugs.

Two species of beetle are responsible for ladybug taint: *Harmonia axyridis,* already mentioned; and a native European species, *Coccinella septempunctata* (seven-spotted lady beetle). These ladybugs take up residence in the grape cluster and end up in the fermentation vat, and when they are stressed (getting crushed and drowned is pretty stressful) they release methoxypyrazines. Just one per vine is enough to taint the wine, and with global warming they are becoming a bigger problem. Affected wines are described as having flavors of greenness, peanuts, and earth.

Clearly, it is advantageous not to let ladybugs into ferments. I recently did some vintage at an Ontario winery where they employed a vibrating sorting table, which all the red-wine grape bunches passed. This particular vintage, they found that quite a few ladybugs had fallen out of the bunches, which otherwise would have ended up in the fermenter. So vibrating sorting tables might be of use for wineries that are working on a small enough scale to make them feasible. But what can be done about these green flavors if they are present? Destemming and minimizing skin contact is important, because most methoxypyrazines are extracted in the first twenty-four hours of maceration, but this is clearly not possible for red wines. Clarification and settling prior to fermentation can make a big difference in reducing levels in the final wine.

Gary Pickering, of Brock University in Ontario, Canada, has worked on this problem for a number of years. He recently published some work on a couple of novel remediation techniques. In his laboratory, he has shown that the use of mMUP (mouse major urinary protein), an odorant-binding protein specific for methoxypyrazines, can reduce levels from 300 ng/L to just 5 ng/L.[2] This protein binds the methoxypyrazines and is then fined out with bentonite. In his experiments, mMUP reduced methoxypyrazine levels by 98 percent, but in wine there's a potential issue with the alcohol changing the structure of this protein and rendering it less effective. In another experiment, he trialed a range of polyethylene-based polymers to see whether these could absorb some of the methoxypyrazines. The three best polymers in the trial each reduced the level by about 40 percent without any real negative sensory impact on the wine, which is a promising result.

Clearly, it's best not to have sky-high levels of methoxypyrazines in wine in the first place, but if you do, it's nice to have a remedial solution. Other potential solutions that have been tried include the use of oak chips, which seem to be effective in reducing the perception of this taint: they appear to mask it with various oak-derived volatile components, such as vanillin and oak lactone.[3] Of course, this is a pretty drastic step to take and will work only with certain wine styles, and for more commercial wines rather than fine wines. The threshold for this taint is lower in red wines that it is in whites, which is an unusual finding. It's probably because green aromas are more normal in white wines than in reds. In Marlborough Sauvignon Blanc, for example, a degree of green is considered normal and appealing.

Interestingly, the concentration of IPMP in the hemolymph of *Harmonia axyridis* has been reported to be a hundred times higher than that in the native *Coccinella septempunctata*. This initially suggests that winegrowers really need to be vigilant in looking for the Asian species and don't need to worry too much about the native one. But Kögel and colleagues have demonstrated that the hemolymph of the European seven-spotted lady beetle is quite capable of tainting wine.[4] Indeed, their paper mentions a personal communication stating that the seven-spot had already affected the taste of some German wines in the 1970s and '80s. In this study, the smell caused by eight beetles per liter of wine was recognized by nearly all panelists in a sensory test, and wines contaminated with the seven-spot showed a stronger taint than those contaminated with the Asian ladybug. In practice, this means that growers should be vigilant about *any* ladybugs getting into the vat.

The same researchers have also done a further study on the sensory thresholds for ladybug taint.[5] They found that the sensory detection threshold for this taint in Pinot Noir was around three beetles per kilogram of grapes; in Riesling it was around four beetles per kilogram. IPMP was detected by half the panelists in a sensory study at a threshold of 1 ng/L (one part per trillion) in Riesling and double this in Pinot Noir (at odds with the finding that the taint is more apparent in reds than in whites).

OTHER SOURCES OF GREENNESS

Methoxypyrazines aren't the only compounds responsible for greenness in wine. A group of C6 aldehydes, which are also described as "green leaf" aldehydes, can contribute these green flavors. These include hexenol and hexenal. The most important is *cis*-3-hexen-1-ol, which smells of cut grass, herbaceous and leafy. Its threshold in wine is around 400 µg/L.

Dimethyl sulfide is a volatile sulfur compound commonly found in wine. It has a range of aromas, depending on its concentration and the wine type, including canned corn, canned tomato, asparagus, and black currant. It can contribute vegetal flavors to wines at higher concentrations. The threshold for detection is 35 µg/L, and it can make a positive contribution at levels up to 100 µg/L. Above this it becomes problematic.

ARE WE TOO SCARED OF GREENNESS?

Greenness is quite acceptable in Sauvignon Blanc, where it is seen as part of the aroma profile of the wine, particularly in New Zealand, where the greenness is nicely countered by exotic fruity aromatics, many of which are contributed by the polyfunctional thiols 3-MH and 3-MHA. But in red wines it's often considered a problem. As a result, winegrowers have frequently waited for any trace of greenness to disappear before harvesting grapes. This has led to advanced harvest dates, with resulting jammy fruit flavors and high alcohol levels in the final wines. Most people would agree that excessive greenness is a problem, but the danger is that in the quest to avoid it, grapes are picked too late, with an attendant loss of freshness and definition in the wine. In the past, subtle green flavors in young red wines were seen as appropriate, particularly for Cabernet Sauvignon, Cabernet Franc, and Merlot. Classic old Bordeaux often had a sappy greenness to it in its youth, and it aged beautifully. It's all about balance and context. Fortunately, many producers are now moving away from extended hang time and looking to pick a bit earlier. Certainly, good viticulture can allow growers to harvest blocks that are more homogeneous, so they don't have strikingly different ripeness levels in the same lot. This can result in a combination of very sweet and green flavors in the wine, which is usually unattractive. But a little sappy, leafy greenness in the right context can be an attractive feature in a red wine. Modern optical sorters can now eliminate single unripe berries, even if they look perfectly ripe to the human eye. This can reduce the green notes in the resulting wine.

PORTUGUESE MILLIPEDE TAINT

There's a new taint, related to ladybug taint, emerging in parts of the McLaren Vale and Adelaide Hills in Australia. It's caused by an imported species, the Portuguese millipede *(Ommatoiulus moreletii),* introduced accidentally at Port Lincoln in the 1950s. The millipedes have thrived because they have no known predators in Australia. They are impossible to control on a large scale, in part because they are mainly active at night. When threatened, they curl into a ball and release chemicals that are extremely aversive to any other organism planning to eat them. The AWRI has looked at these chemicals because they are implicated in wine taints—if millipedes get into the vat during winemaking, they'll release them. And some wines have been sent in with a taint that's thought to be millipede-derived.

BROWN MARMORATED STINK BUG

Endemic to China, Taiwan, Japan, and Korea, the exotically named brown marmorated stink bug *(Halyomorpha halys)* was accidentally introduced into the United States in the late 1990s. It has also made its way to Europe and South America. It's a big problem in fruit orchards. In wine grapes, it can cause crop losses through its feeding behavior, but there is more concern about the sensory effects of making wine from grapes with these insects present in or on the bunches. Tridecane, dodecane, trans-2-decenal, and trans-2-undecen-1-ol have been identified as volatile compounds released by the stink bug. It produces a musty, coriander/cilantro aroma in wines, particularly reds, and is an increasing problem in many wine regions, especially in China where it is native. Evidence suggests that just a few of these bugs per cluster can take the main aromatic taint, trans-2-decenal, above threshold levels.[6]

While it is unclear exactly how much wine is affected by ladybug taint, this is an issue that winegrowers need to be aware of, especially in an age of climate change and unpredictable harvest weather that could lead to some seasons having a large ladybug population in the vineyard. Vigilance needs to be shown, and growers should be keen to avoid letting these insects into fermentation vats.

CHAPTER FOURTEEN

Mousiness

- **What is it?** A distinct flavor/aroma of mouse cages that can't be smelled until the wine is in the mouth. It's slightly sweet and earthy—not musty, but not completely clean.
- **What is its flavor impact?** It's a strange taint, in that it isn't detectable on the nose but appears on the palate after the wine has been in the mouth for a few seconds or even sometimes a bit longer. It is experienced retro-nasally if the pH of your saliva is able to increase the pH of the wine sufficiently.
- **What causes it?** It's thought to be caused mainly by lactic acid bacteria, but it's possible that it may be formed chemically too.
- **Is it always bad?** Yes, although some people don't find it offensive and can tolerate it better than others, and some can't spot it at all.
- **How can it be prevented?** By avoiding high-pH fermentations and using adequate levels of SO_2.

· **How common is it?** It's common in natural wines, especially reds, where the pH is a bit higher.

Mousiness is a taint that seems to be on the rise, but it's a complicated wine fault to deal with. This is because it doesn't smell of anything until the wine is in your mouth. According to the AWRI, it used to be detected quite rarely, but over the past few years they've started encountering it more often. This is put down to the move by some towards more natural winemaking techniques, in which winemakers are using less and less SO_2 or adding it only very late in the winemaking process. It is also thought that working with higher pH in red wines is a contributing factor. I have certainly encountered this fault quite a bit in natural-wine fairs. The AWRI lists five potential risk factors: high-solids ferment, extended lees aging, higher pH, oxidative aging, and minimal clarification/filtration.

The main chemical responsible for the taint is 2-acetyltetrahydropyridine. Other compounds responsible are 2-ethyltetrahydropyridine and 2-acetylpyrroline. These are not aromatic at wine pH, but once you get the wine in your mouth it begins to change pH, to the point that you can smell (retro-nasally) the typical mousiness signature of caged mice and crackers. The wine may taste fine when you first sip it, but after a while, on the finish, you get this mousy character emerging. If you are tasting a lineup of several wines, it is sometimes a few minutes later that you will experience mousiness. This is presumably because tasting wines in succession lowers the pH of the mouth environment, and it takes a while for the saliva to raise it. In this case, you don't know which of the wines was mousy.

But there's a further twist. Up to a third of the population aren't able to spot it at all. So, some winemakers may be bottling wines that they think are fine, while two-thirds of their customers find them unacceptable.

It has long been believed that the main cause of mousiness is microbial. Lactic acid bacteria are considered the culprits, mainly *Lactobacillus hilgardii.* Also cited are *L. brevis* and *Oenococcus oeni.* Some texts implicate *L. plantarum* as well, but because it lacks the necessary biochemical pathways, it must be a minor player at best. Some texts contend that the rogue yeast *Brettanomyces* is able to produce mousiness. However, the AWRI have looked at a lot of brett-affected wines and dispute this. "During our extensive work and tastings with brett," says Peter Godden, "we never saw a bretty wine that was also mousy—and we looked at a lot of extremely bretty wines." Oxygen is also thought to be involved in the process.

It can also be produced chemically, by the the process of hyperoxidation, when hydrogen peroxide is used to remove SO_2 from juice or wine. This is sometimes carried out with sparkling base wines, where too much SO_2 can prevent the secondary fermentation in bottle needed to produce the bubbles.

But recent research from Austria suggests that 2-acetyltetrahydropyridine could be formed by the Maillard reaction from methylglyoxal and proline. This research is quite preliminary, though, and more work needs to be done to confirm it.

Overall, though, mousiness is still quite a mysterious fault. You can't measure it easily in wine (other than by sensory analysis with an experienced taster), and there are no remedial steps other than blending an affected wine away. Besides the portion of the population who can't detect it, it's likely that some people don't really notice it, or do notice it and don't mind it, judging from the success of some mousy wines in natural-wine fairs.

One winegrower who has been trying hard to get to grips with this fault is Eric Texier, who works in the northern Rhône. He says that *goût de souris*—mousiness—is his main research subject. "I have no idea what causes it," he says. "I have been working on it for ten years now and I still don't have a conclusion. It is a bit like premox [premature oxidation, a problem that has afflicted white Burgundy since the mid-1990s]. We think we understand it but we don't."

What Texier has found, though, is that a small addition of SO_2 during fermentation—just 10 ppm is adequate—will stop it. "What is unusual with mousiness is that the best insurance against biological trouble—low pH—doesn't help, which is extremely weird. It might need some chemistry to explain it, not only biology. For all other microbiological problems, low pH always helps." He adds, "You find mouse in Champagne and Aligoté," citing two wines that usually have very low pH.

Texier believes that for mousiness to develop, there needs to be a conjunction of a specific strain of yeast with a specific strain of lactic acid bacteria and also a specific chemistry. "But we don't know exactly." He adds that high pH and high alcohol are less likely to result in mousiness than low pH and low alcohol. "Some people think you need pyridine as a precursor, but it's pyridine plus something. It's a chemical reaction that gives it, but I have no proof."

Texier gets together with other vignerons working with low SO_2, and they share their experiences of mousiness, in a bid to understand it better. "We have cases of it appearing in bottle after sterile fermentation," he adds. "Perhaps the precurors are microbial, but the final reaction is purely chemical." In 2015, Texier lost 20 hL of wine, which had to go to distillation, because of mousiness. In 2016, he lost none.

"Old vines never give me mouse," says Texier. "Some vineyards never do. We almost never have mouse in rainy vintages, especially if we have rain just before vintage." He estimates that among winegrowers who work with no SO_2, 20–25 percent of wine is tainted with mousiness.

With the growing popularity of natural wine, expect this to be a fault that attracts increasing attention.

CHAPTER FIFTEEN

Faults of Malolactic Fermentation

- **What is it?** Lactic acid bacteria have a significant sensory impact on wine, and some of these effects can be negative.
- **What is its impact?** They can produce diacetyl, biogenic amines, volatile sulfur compounds, volatile acidity, and ethyl carbamate, among other compounds. Some of these don't have a flavor, but instead have health implications.
- **What causes it?** Malolactic fermentation is common in wine, and the bacteria involved differ quite a bit in their potential sensory impact.
- **Is it always bad?** These bacteria produce a very wide range of sensory effects, some of which are positive and some negative. It's a complex picture. For example, diacetyl—which has buttery, dairy flavors—is liked by some tasters and despised by others.
- **How can it be prevented?** By monitoring the malolactic fermentation. It's now possible to inoculate with selected strains of bacteria to avoid some of the problems.

· **How common is it?** Excessive levels of diacetyl aren't uncommon. The sensory impact of lactic acid bacteria has only recently begun to be appreciated, so it's hard to say.

Bacteria are important in winemaking, but it's only fairly recently that their role has been understood to any degree. They can contribute to the wine fault of volatile acidity (discussed in chapter 5), but they are also involved in the second fermentation that takes place in almost all red wines and many whites, called malolactic fermentation (MLF). This involves the softening of acidity by converting the more aggressive malic acid into the gentler lactic acid, but it's now becoming clear that MLF also has a significant sensory impact, which can be beneficial or harmful.

The first mention of MLF is thought to be in a book from 1837 by Freiherr von Babo in which he referred to a second fermentation occurring in some wines in spring, as the temperatures began to rise. This resulted in the release of carbon dioxide and renewed turbidity in the wine. In 1866, the celebrated scientist Louis Pasteur isolated bacteria from wine for the first time, but he considered all bacteria in wine to be spoilage organisms. A breakthrough came in 1891, when Hermann Müller Thurgau first proposed that the commonly observed acid reduction in fermenting wine could be due to bacterial activity. This was a bold suggestion, because at the time this change in acid levels was thought to be caused by tartaric acid precipitation. He went on to do some important work over the next couple of decades in collaboration with a fellow Swiss researcher called Osterwalder. In 1939, famous French wine scientist Emile Peynaud wrote an important paper on the role of malic acid in the musts and wines in Bordeaux, pointing out that the absence of MLF was a quality-limiting factor in these wines. "Not only is the acid make-up of the wine completely changed," he stated, "but [MLF] has an impact on the perfume of these wines and even diminishes the intensity of the color and changes its shade. It is not exaggerating to say that without malolactic fermentation, there would hardly be any great reds of Bordeaux."

Although yeast cultures were starting to become available, no one had yet successfully cultured the lactic acid bacteria responsible for the conversion of malic to lactic acid, with its corresponding softening of acidity. This was to wait until the late 1950s.

Malic acid is present in large quantities in unripe grapes. As grapes ripen, its concentration diminishes, and by harvest time it constitutes around a tenth to a quarter of total grape acids. The other two significant organic acids in wine are tartaric acid (the main one) and citric acid (present in lesser quantities). The exact amount of malic acid will depend on the climate, with a range of 2.0–6.5 g/L (tartaric acid is found at 5–10 g/L), although malic acid levels of 15 g/L have been reported in grapes harvested from very cool climates. It has quite a sharp taste. Before veraison takes place, malic acid is the main grape acid and can occur at 25 g/L, but this diminishes rapidly with the last stage of ripening. During MLF the lactic acid bacteria convert the malic acid to lactic acid, which is a softer-tasting acid and also a less powerful one. So there's a pH shift and a loss of acidity with this second fermentation, the degree of which will depend on how much malic acid was present in the grapes in the first place. Malolactic fermentation happens in almost all red wines. Whether a winemaker allows it to occur in whites is usually a style decision on their part.

But there is a lot more to MLF than simply this acidic conversion. Just as yeasts have a significant sensory impact above and beyond simply converting sugar to alcohol, lactic acid bacteria change the flavor of wine in ways that are only now becoming really appreciated, as scientists take a closer look at the activity of these microbes. The sensory impact of lactic acid bacteria can be both positive and negative, and it largely depends on the strain of bacteria doing the fermentation, the presence of certain substrates in the wine, and the conditions under which the fermentation takes place.

The four genera (a genus is the level of classification just above species) of lactic acid bacteria found in wine are *Oenococcus, Leuconostoc, Lactobacillus,* and *Pediococcus.* One species, *Oenococcus oeni,* is of particular interest. Because it produces the best results, it's the species that winemakers want to carry out this second fermentation. And it usually does so, because it is pretty resistant to the hostile conditions found in wines just after alcoholic fermentation has finished—much more so than the other three genera, which tend to grow only when the pH is a little higher.

Feeding off any sugars that remain in the wine after the yeasts have finished (yeasts leave a bit of hexose and pentose sugars), the lactic acid bacteria grow in numbers. The bacteria need less than 1 g/L of sugars to create a biomass sufficient to carry out MLF. Alongside this activity, they are also able to do the conversion of malic to lactic acid, but it's worth emphasizing that this is just one of their metabolic activities. During the course of their growth they are able to secrete a range of flavor compounds into the wine. This is where bacteria have the potential for enhancing quality or affecting it negatively. It is instructive to taste experimental wines inoculated with different strains of cultured malolactic bacteria. This sort of comparison shows the degree to which MLF can change the taste of the wine, in addition to modifying the acidity. But there's very little written on the subject, and most winemakers allow MLF to happen spontaneously, trusting that they are going to get a decent strain of malolactic bacteria that will carry out the MLF.

VOLATILE ACIDITY

Lactic acid bacteria produce acetic acid by metabolizing sugars, which will increase volatile acidity. The degree to which volatile acidity is increased depends on how much sugar they metabolize, so this is a potential concern when MLF starts while the yeasts haven't quite finished their job. Again, this increase in volatile acidity is quite strain dependent. As well as degrading malic acid, some strains of lactic acid bacteria also degrade tartaric acid. Fortunately, only a very few strains can do this. It's very bad when it happens—Pasteur called this *tourne disease*. However, it is now quite common for winemakers to co-inoculate with bacteria and yeast at the same time, especially when the aim is to produce fruity, youthful red wines. The results can be very impressive. Clearly, the bacteria are working here in a sugar-rich environment. The strains of yeast and bacteria need to be chosen carefully, but perhaps the worry about bacteria working when there is sugar present is overstated.

DIACETYL

One of the most well-known sensory impacts of lactic acid bacteria is the production of diacetyl (2,3-butanedione). This has an odor detection threshold of 0.2 mg/L in white wines and 2.8 mg/L in reds. It's formed by lactic acid bacteria from citric acid, which is one of the main organic acids in wine. Diacetyl has a distinctive buttery, creamy character and can be attractive at small levels. But higher levels of diacetyl aren't pleasant and can be considered a fault. In fact, there are some circumstances where *detectable* diacetyl is undesirable. The factors favoring diacetyl production are the presence of oxygen, high concentrations of citric acid and sugar, temperatures below 18°C, and the removal of yeast cells before MLF. The levels can be reduced by the presence of viable yeast cells and by addition of SO_2 (but not enough to inhibit all the bacteria). Diacetyl can react with cysteine (an amino acid containing sulfur) to produce thiazole, which smells of toast, popcorn, and hazelnut.

VOLATILE SULFUR COMPOUNDS

A particularly interesting contribution to wine flavor from lactic acid bacteria is the production of volatile sulfur compounds (VSCs), the subject of chapter 6. These are produced by the metabolism of the sulfur-containing amino acids cysteine and methionine, and the VSCs that result can be good or bad, depending on the context. These are the compounds implicated in reduction problems in wines.

ACROLEIN

Acrolein, a bitter-tasting compound, is produced by some lactic acid bacteria strains by the degradation of glycerol. It's undesirable at any level, but fortunately only a few strains produce it.

BIOGENIC AMINES

One of the most talked-about byproducts of MLF is the formation of biogenic amines. All fermented products contain them, but malolactic bacteria are capable of producing reasonably high levels. They are formed by the decarboxylation of amino acids, and the major ones found in wine are histamine, tyramine, putrescine, and phenylethylamine. They can have a range of effects on people sensitive to them, including headaches, breathing difficulties, hypertension or hypotension, allergic reactions, and palpitations. People differ in sensitivity, but the presence of biogenic amines in wine is always undesirable.

Not all strains of lactic acid bacteria are able to decarboxylate amino acids. The higher the wine's pH, the more complex the range of bacterial species that will grow in it; as a result, there will usually be higher levels of biogenic amines. And white wines—which usually have a lower pH—tend to have lower levels of biogenic amines. Although sulfites are often blamed for allergic reactions to wine, biogenic amines are much more likely to be responsible, although this hasn't been proved conclusively. Using selected strains of lactic acid bacteria to inoculate for MLF is one way to reduce the risk of biogenic amines in wines. Currently there are no regulations for biogenic amine levels in wine, but this could change.

ETHYL CARBAMATE

Biogenic amines aren't the worst thing that certain strains of bacteria produce. Ethyl carbamate is a carcinogen that's found in many foods and drinks, and it's formed through reactions between alcohol and a precursor such as citrulline, urea, or carbamyl phosphate. The main contributor to ethyl carbamate levels in wine is urea that is formed by yeasts from the degradation of arginine, but even after alcoholic fermentation some arginine (0.1–2.3 g/L) remains in the wine, and lactic acid bacteria can produce citrulline as an intermediate in the degradation process of arginine. The United States has regulations that set the maximum level of ethyl carbamate in wine at 15 µg/L. The maximum allowed in Canada is 30 µg/L, and the EU has no uniform maximum level. Typically, wine contains around 10 µg/L and fortified wines contain around 60 µg/L, but these levels can vary. You really don't want ethyl carbamate in your wines.

POSITIVE EFFECTS

One positive effect of lactic acid bacteria is that some strains are thought to have glycosidase activity. Many of the flavor molecules in grape juice are in a chemical state where they need to be converted during fermentation to be active. A glycosidase is an enzyme that removes sugar groups, and in this case it can hydrolyze sugar-bound monoterpenes to release them as volatile aromatic monoterpenes. There is also some evidence that lactic acid bacteria are able to synthesize esters, which are fruity-smelling compounds, but this needs to be verified further.

Lactic acid bacteria are able to remove green flavors from wine. The reduction of vegetative/green grassy aromas that can occur during MLF is thought to be through the metabolism of aldehydes, such as hexenal, that contribute to these green flavors (along with methoxypyrazines). Lactic acid bacteria are also thought to be able to improve the body of a wine—for example, through the production of polyols and polysaccharides.

Of all the flavor impacts of MLF, the main one is the change in acidity, which is quite significant. It usually increases pH (makes the wine less acidic) by 0.1–0.3 units and reduces total acidity by 1–3 g/L.

Depending on which country you are working in, most MLFs will be spontaneous, but it is becoming increasingly common to inoculate with bacterial cultures (in Australia, for example, this is now the norm). These come in different forms. There are freeze-dried cultures that need to be reawakened, making a starter culture with which to inoculate the wine, and there are now active dried cultures that can be added together with the yeast. Cultured bacteria are a bit fussier than cultured yeasts, and they need to be handled carefully. Previously it was thought that the only safe time to inoculate was after alcoholic fermentation was complete, because of the risk of volatile acidity increasing (if the bacteria are eating lots of sugar) and the risk that an incompatibility between the bacteria and yeasts might cause fermentation to stick. Now, though, co-inoculation with compatible strains of bacteria and yeasts is commonplace. The advantage is that as long as the two microbe strains work well together, the result is fruitier wines (especially reds), in part because any diacetyl produced by the bacteria is used by the yeasts. As such, co-inoculation is particularly advised for less expensive, fruit-forward red wines, with the added bonus of no risk period between the end of alcoholic fermentation and the beginning of MLF.

It is clear that the lactic acid bacteria that carry out MLF have a significant sensory impact on wine, and that as well as having the potential to improve wine quality, there is a real risk of faults developing during this second fermentation. Generally speaking, working with lower pH levels is the safest way to make wine from a microbial standpoint. Winemaking at higher pH, say above 3.8, carries with it lots of risk, and unwanted bacterial growth is much more likely to occur. There's a lot that remains to be discovered about bacteria in wine, and this is surely a topic that hasn't been investigated as much as it merits.

CHAPTER SIXTEEN

Laboratory Testing for
Wine Faults

One of the key tools for modern winemaking is information about what is going on with a wine both during and after fermentation. Winemakers need to be able to identify faults that are developing early on, while there is still time to take remedial action, and sometimes just tasting the wine isn't enough. This is especially the case where winemaking is more low-intervention, because of the various risks involved. "If you were an extremely large winery in the Central Valley and were willing to harvest grapes early, use a high level of SO_2, and sterile filter before bottling, you could make wine without any analysis," says Gordon Burns of ETS Laboratories.

> But if you don't want to add SO_2 or [want to add] minimal amounts, and want to use a native ferment, it's like you are a parent with a small child walking near to the edge of the cliff. You need to have your hand on their collar. People who are most non-interventionist need to have more knowledge than people working at a more industrial scale. Many of them recognize that, and a significant part of our work comes from those who are trying to do the least.

Winemakers not only want the basic information about levels of SO_2 (the most commonly carried out winemaking analysis), acids (volatile and total/titratable), pH, alcohol, and sugars; they also want more exotic analyses such as phenolics, volatile sulfur compounds, and the presence of spoilage microbes such as *Brettanomyces*. Typically a winery will use a two-step approach to getting this sort of information. In addition to having their own laboratory, they will also use third-party commercial laboratories for analyses that require more expensive equipment, or specialized staff, or techniques that just aren't possible to implement in house.

But things are changing fast, in terms of the cost and capability of analytical equipment that wineries might buy for their own labs, and also in terms of the sorts of analyses that are possible in commercial labs. "The things formerly available only in commercial or very large labs are finding their way down to mid-tier producers and are now being adopted," says Burns.

Some fifteen years ago, the emergence of affordable spectral analysis made a big impact on the analyses that wineries could do in house, and also on the ability of commercial labs to offer cheap analysis for winery clients. Spectral analyses have been very effective in helping winemakers understand what is going on with their wines and thus make decisions that reduce the incidence of faults and result in enhanced quality. They are based on the visual, near-infrared and mid-infrared spectra. Their advantage is that they can do multiple analyses on single samples in just a minute or two, with no expensive reagents. Previously, wine labs had to do these sorts of analyses separately, and they took much more time and involved expensive chemicals.

Now, though, these tools are available to look at the composition of grapes, must, and fermenting wine. They can inform decisions such as time of harvest, determination of fruit quality (for remunerating growers and for choosing the destination of grapes in the winery), and whether or not to supplement the must (e.g., with nitrogen or acid). They also aid in monitoring the progress of fermentation. One of the most widely used spectral analyzers is the FOSS WineScan, which operates by Fourier-transform infrared spectroscopy, looking at the near-infrared spectrum. This shines an infrared beam through a wine sample and then analyzes the spectrum that is produced. Typically, this is used to look at ethanol level, pH, volatile acidity, and titratable acidity. Since 2011, it is also able to measure free and total SO_2 level. It is possible to run 120 samples an hour through a machine like this.

Machines also exist that look at mid-infrared. This can be used for similar analyses but is better at looking at the yeast assimilable nitrogen (YAN) content of musts. This is a very useful measure because if the level is too low, yeasts can struggle and produce off-flavors. This information allows winemakers to make informed choices about potential supplementation. Traditionally, YAN measurements would have required specialist equipment and would have been much slower. Once a machine has been purchased, spectral analysis is cheap and quick, and it has lowered the cost of commercial analyses too. As such, it has been a major step in reducing the incidence of wine faults. It is not perfect, and there is a need for regular calibration, but the advantages of speed and cost usually outweigh the disadvantages.

One of the big changes in recent years has been the adoption of molecular biology approaches. In July 2016, on a visit to the AWRI, one of the scientists I interviewed was yeast researcher Dr. Anthony Borneman. Typically, in the past, the way to see what yeasts were present involved the use of plating. You would take a sterile Petri dish with a nutrient medium and a small sample of soil or wine (depending on what you were looking at). Then you'd allow whatever was present in the soil or wine to grow on the nutrient medium in big enough quantities to identify it. "Plating gets you just one percent of what is present in the soils," says Borneman. "In wine it's better, but you still miss a lot." But now DNA sequencing is becoming much more affordable and rapid, and this has the potential to tell you about everything that is present.

Borneman showed me a small USB-powered device, three inches long. This is the MinION (pronounced "min-eye-on"), produced by a UK-based company called Oxford Nanopore. It's a portable DNA sequencer that has the potential to open up incredible new opportunities for studying what is actually happening in the winery. Winemakers can use it to do real-time sequencing of microbes present in the winery and the vineyard. How does this work? DNA consists of long chains of four different subunits, called nucleotides or bases, usually known by a one-letter code: A, T, C, and G (adenine, thymine, cytosine, and guanine, respectively). The sequence of these bases forms genes, which then are translated to form proteins. The human genome, for example, consists of some three billion base pairs and twenty thousand genes. Since next-generation sequencing methods emerged in 2005, the cost of sequencing has fallen dramatically, from around $1,000 per million base pairs to under ten cents. The cost of sequencing has been driven down by a factor of ten every eighteen months, which is a staggering rate of change.

The MinION makes use of a new technology called nanopore sequencing. A nanopore is a tiny protein with a hole in the middle of it, which sits inside an artificial membrane. An electric current is applied to the nanopore, and as a strand of DNA passes through the nanopore, the density of the current will change according to the sequence of the DNA. This portable sequencer can cheaply and reliably sequence bacteria and yeast genomes. Other low-cost benchtop machines are made by Miseq and Illumina.

"DNA sequencing is easy," says Borneman. The hurdles here are sample preparation (which isn't trivial) and the process of making sense of the raw data to produce something actionable. It's feasible that soon, wineries so inclined could monitor, in real time, the winery and vineyard to see which microbes are present, using one of these devices and some decent software on their laptops. This is quite exciting, and it would have been like science fiction a decade ago. It could enable winemakers to intervene in real time in fermentations because they would know exactly which microbes were present. It would also enable viticulturists to know what was happening with microbes in the vineyard: for example, they could see whether fungal pathogens were showing resistance to certain agrochemical classes. Genomic differences in yeast strains could be used as molecular markers of traits, which could rapidly increase the speed of strain selection. Aside from lab testing, other applications of cheap sequencing could be to screen consumers for flavor preferences (increasingly, the genetic contribution to flavor perception is being revealed) or to test winemakers for specific anosmias (inability to smell certain molecules) that could lead them to miss certain faults or taints in wine.

While DNA sequencing isn't yet a mainstream technology for wineries, another DNA method has become widespread and affordable. This is PCR (polymerase chain reaction) analysis, a powerful technique that has changed how laboratories and even wineries analyze for *Brettanomyces*. Polymerase chain reaction was invented in the early 1980s. Although the concept behind it is quite simple, it relies on an unusually resilient enzyme called Taq polymerase, which was isolated from bugs growing in a hot spring in Yellowstone National Park. The idea behind PCR is to take two primers, which are bits of DNA that identify a specific sequence. These primers are put into a small test tube with the four DNA bases, the Taq polymerase enzyme, and the DNA sample to be tested, which can be very small. The test tube is then placed in a thermal cycler, which heats the sample to 90°C (enough to uncouple the DNA strand), then cools it to 50°C for the primers to fuse on the now single strands of DNA, and then warms it again for the DNA strands to reform and replicate through the action of the polymerase. This cycle is repeated, each time producing new strands of DNA as defined by the primers. After many repeats, the result is millions or even billions of copies of the bit of DNA of interest. The key to this is having a DNA polymerase that can withstand such high temperatures: as proteins, most enzymes lose their structure above 45°C.

This technology has found many uses, the most famous of which is in forensic science, where only the tiniest bit of DNA is needed to produce results. For wine, it has been exploited by Invisible Sentinel, a company whose most well-known product, VinoBRETT, is powered by a technology they have named Veriflow. The basis for this PCR test is primers based on a small strand of DNA from *Brettanomyces bruxellensis*. Traditionally, testing for brett has involved plating, a procedure that takes seven to ten days. That timescale isn't really fast enough for winemakers to be reactive to any problems. The new PCR-based tests provide results within four hours. Gordon Burns of ETS Laboratories is very upbeat about these new technologies. "The biggest thing in ETS is molecular biology and microbiology, using specific probes and real-time PCR," he says. "If you asked [ETS] as recently as five to six years ago to look for microbes in wine, about 10 percent was molecular biology and 90 percent was traditional plating. This has now inverted to 90 percent using molecular probes. This is so important because of the limitations of plating."

As well as taking a long time, plating is also limited to looking for actively growing bugs. One of the problems with brett is thought to be the "viable but nonculturable" state (although some controversy surrounds this, as discussed in chapter 3). This is when brett cells enter a sort of limbo state in which they are still alive but aren't dividing or metabolizing; if conditions change, they are able to start growing again. They are also smaller than regular cells and so can pass more easily through filters. This makes them particularly problematic, and only PCR is able to spot them.

Burns says that for these molecular tests, ETS do a two-day turnover, but often it turns out to be a same-day service. "So it's in time for winemakers to do something about it," he says. "It becomes predictive, not forensic. All microbiology in winemaking from the time of Pasteur has been forensic: why did this wine spoil? Now techniques are fast." And if customers have VinoBRETT in house, it's even quicker—but the potential issue here is reliability of results. In a commercial lab, there are quality-control procedures; the risk with taking this in house is false negatives, where your wine is declared clean when it isn't.

Sample preparation is simple: the wine just needs to be centrifuged. Then there are two-and-a-half hours of thermocycling, after which the sample is poured onto a test cassette window for a readout, much as you might do with a pregnancy test. However, unlike with pregnancy, you can have no brett, a little bit of brett, or a lot of brett—it's semiquantitative. The cost of bringing Vino-BRETT in house isn't crazy: the reagents for twenty-four tests cost $840, and the thermocycler costs around $3,500. A centrifuge is also needed, but many labs will already have one. However, while in-house testing like this might cost $45 per sample, the lab fee for the same test of around $60 per sample isn't a lot higher, considering the enhanced accuracy it offers.

Aside from DNA technology, the other significant technology opening up new analytic possibilities is cheaper and more accurate GC–MS (gas chromatography–mass spectrometry). This powerful analytic technique allows detection of tiny quantities of compounds of interest present in wine. "Over the last twelve to fifteen years, we have gone through six generations and iterations of GC–MS," says Burns. "As the instrumentation gets better, accuracy gets better and reportable concentrations get lower every two or three years." An interesting related technology is MS–MS, where MS is followed by another MS that hones in on specific compounds of interest, rather than trying to identify unknown compounds. "This is hugely important," says Burns, "because it allows the development of practical analyses previously only available in the research laboratories, such as low-level methoxypyrazines and looking at haloanisoles and halophenols in cooperage oak."

One very interesting application is to use a technique called *cryofocusing*, where headspace over a wine sample is focused by chilling the inlet to −90°C. Then the inlet is warmed, and GC–MS with a chemoluminescence detector is used to look at volatile sulfur compounds in the wine, which are responsible for reduction problems. This is of intense current interest, and affordable analysis of volatile sulfur compounds is of great interest to winemakers. "If winemakers are forthcoming they would put this in the top three or four issues," says Burns. "There are many mysteries still involved with sulfide formation and remedying things." Looking at a panel of volatile sulfur compounds requires the use of a commercial laboratory. Burns continues:

> Only two wineries in the USA have the capabilities in house to look at sulfides. People use this analysis routinely through the winemaking process to detect disulfides in particular. Methyl mercaptan is a particularly problematic volatile sulfur compound, with a very low sensory threshold of around 2 ppb [the same as μg/L]. If you oxidize it the wine will stop smelling. Winemakers assume that this is because it has blown off, but actually it is because it has been oxidized to dimethyl disulfide, which has a detection threshold of 10–15 ppb. It stops smelling but it is still there, and later it may hydrolyze, and you get the smelly one back. This is because disulfide bonds aren't stable. People say they had a horrid smell and the wine was reduced, so "I splashed the heck out of it and it smelled better. We bottled it and it's stinky again. What happened?" There is a pool of disulfides still present and the single ethyl or methyl mercaptan is present. Modern tools allow us to find the disulfides. [To deal with them] you bump the free SO_2 up a bit higher, use ascorbic acid, and the two cause the disulfide bond to break, to release the single sulfur form, which is addressable by copper.

Whether a winery decides to bring some of these new technologies in house or to make use of analysis services from commercial laboratories will depend on the perceived value of this sort of information, the size of the winery, and the skill set of the staff. But the good news is that technologies that were previously available only through expensive third-party laboratories are now in reach of winery labs and offer a valuable insight into what is taking place in the winery. These tools, when used correctly, can do away with the need for defensive winemaking.

CHAPTER SEVENTEEN

Conclusions

Wine faults seem to be less common than they used to be. I remember buying cheap supermarket wine as a student on a budget in the early 1990s. Some of it was really foul, and faults were frequent. With the exception of cork taint, these days it seems rare to find a commercial, bottled wine that has a clear-cut, unambiguous fault. But that's not to say that faults have been completely eradicated (and later in this chapter we'll hear from Sam Harrop, who thinks that in some categories, faults are rising).

More common than clear-cut faults are wines in which quality has been lost through the presence of fault compounds at levels that detract from the wine. These are wines that are a bit reduced, or have some brett, or have a bit of oxidation or volatile acidity, or have a combination of these problems—enough to strip character from the wine, or obscure terroir, or diminish drinking pleasure. Then there are wines with too much buttery diacetyl from malolactic fermentation or too much sweet vanilla and coconut flavor from inappropriate oak use (can this be considered a fault?), or that have too much eucalypt character, or a bit of smoke taint. Quality can also be lost when there is the presence of what, in some contexts, are fault compounds, but they take the wine away from the style goals of the winemaker or the expectations of the market. For example, some mineral-like reductive notes on a white Burgundy might be acceptable, whereas on a commercial Sauvignon Blanc they would not be. It is far from clear-cut.

In November 2016, I succeeded my colleague Sam Harrop as cochair of the International Wine Challenge (IWC), in charge of monitoring wine faults. The IWC is one of the largest wine competitions in the world, and each year some fifteen thousand different wines are entered. More than twenty thousand bottles are opened during the two-stage judging process, and any that the panels consider faulty are sent to me to have a look at and catalogue. Now that I have done this for two tranches of the competition (twelve days of judging in all), I have even more admiration for Sam's job over the previous six years. He's had to catalogue a lot of faulty wines.

While the panel chairs of the IWC have proved themselves to be good tasters, and their performance is closely monitored each year, my initial impression is that even skilled wine professionals sometimes misdiagnose faults or see faults that aren't there. (Misdiagnosis of cork taint, for example, is simple to show by opening a second bottle and doing a comparison; if the second wine tastes the same as the first slightly suspicious bottle, it is unlikely to be cork taint.) My experience has also confirmed that the boundaries of most wine faults aren't clearly defined. Many wines are somewhat diminished because they haven't been made very carefully, but while they may show some slight evidence of oxidation or brett, for example, they can't really be considered faulty, in the sense that this is a wine that demonstrates a particular fault. They may still be of adequate commercial quality. Also, as noted in several of the preceding chapters, people differ in the level at which they find fault compounds to be a problem (more on this below).

The full results from several years of the recently instituted faults clinic at the IWC aren't yet publicly available (the IWC is working with the AWRI to commercialize these), but some findings have been made public.[1] Overall, from 2007 to 2016, some hundred thousand bottles were opened at the IWC, and the faulty wines were logged by Sam Harrop. The overall rejection rates (not the same as the rate of faults, of course) over this period have been 0.9 percent for cork taint, 0.9 percent for reduction, and 1 percent for oxidation. The older the wine entered, the higher the rejection rate. It needs to be noted that well over one-third of entries were sealed with alternative closures; among cork-sealed wines, the rejection rates for cork taint have been higher than the overall rate—for example, 1.7 percent in 2006, 1.8 percent in 2015, and 1.2 percent in 2016 (although there are confounders, other than cork performance alone, that could explain this result). Around 30 percent of entries are sealed with screw caps, and interestingly, these don't show higher rejection rates than cork-sealed wines for reductive characters.

PERCEIVING FAULTS

Tasters are not measuring devices. Our perception of wine is created, in part, by the brain: past experience, knowledge, and expectations can change the nature of perception, as can the environment in which the wine is sampled. Add to this interindividual differences in perception, and we can see that people might differ markedly in the way they perceive certain fault compounds. And indeed, thresholds for fault and taint molecules are known to differ greatly among groups of tasters. One of the main reasons for this is that we all have different repertoires of olfactory receptors. Altogether, we have around four hundred functional olfactory receptors (we have around a thousand olfactory receptor genes, but more than half are nonfunctioning in humans), but we are able to distinguish a much larger number of different smells. The exact mechanism by which olfactory receptors recognize aroma molecules, and how the signal they create is translated into the perception of smell, is somewhat mysterious. Suffice to say, people differ in their receptor repertoire and, as a result, differ in their ability to smell certain compounds. In some cases, a specific anosmia exists and some people simply can't smell a molecule at all. One example of this that is highly relevant to wine faults is the problem of mousiness—30 percent of people just don't detect it. I've heard of experiences where someone has opened a bottle, they've rejected it as mousy, but their friend has happily drunk the rest. Then there are phenomena such as desensitization and cross-adaptation. A taster might be good at spotting something as they begin tasting, but then after they have been exposed to it a number of times in quick succession, they are unable to smell it until they have had a decent break. This is a big issue in wine judging.

If you wear colored sunglasses, your visual system adapts to their tint; and when you take them off, everything you see has a strange color cast that takes a little while to disappear. A similar sort of adaptation takes place with the sense of smell, and it is called *desensitization*. In a familiar example, we can enter a room or a home and find it noticeably smelly, but after a while we get used to the smell. This is an important ability, because the strong smell would otherwise override subtler smells. It's not a complete adaptation, because particularly powerful smells are merely dampened down. *Cross-adaptation* occurs when the process of adaptation to smell *x* causes some adaptation to smell *y*. While desensitization is problematic for wine tasting, cross-adaptation is a greater hazard. If there is a recurring or prolonged smell in the tasting room, people become desensitized to that smell. Together, these phenomena explain why some winemakers might have "cellar palate," failing to detect taints or faults simply because they have grown used to them.

One other fact that needs to be considered is that wine is a complex matrix, and the presence of some compounds—even at sub-threshold levels—can influence the way that other compounds are perceived. One of the great illustrations of this is provided by the work by Vicente Ferreira and his colleagues, who looked at the effect of the nonvolatile matrix on wine aromatics. If you take a red wine, strip it of aromas, and add the aromatics from a white wine, it still smells like a red wine. And the opposite also applies.

Together, these observations show that we should be cautious about simplistic explanations and approaches to wine faults. The reality is far more complex than a binary distinction of faulty versus correct. You can't say, for example, that a wine containing *x* micrograms of 4-ethylphenol per liter is not bretty, but a wine with more than that is bretty.

There's also the issue of learning. We learn to like wine; our tastes are not simply innate. It's entirely possible that some people grow to like wines with high levels of *Brettanomyces* through repeated exposure to them, just as we can grow to love stinky cheeses that we initially found quite aversive. I don't know anyone who has grown to love musty or cork-tainted wine, but plenty of people appreciate bretty or oxidized wines that others would describe as faulty. There's a phenomenon known as *mere exposure*. This is where our liking for something increases as we are repeatedly exposed to it, and it is thought to be very important in preference acquisition. One example of mere exposure would be in interpersonal relations, when you find someone more pleasing and likable on repeated encounters. This has been studied for smell: do we like odors because they are familiar?

One of the most interesting studies in this area was carried out by Sylvain Delplanque and colleagues in 2015. They gave participants several odors and asked them to rate each odor's pleasantness, intensity, and familiarity. They found that neutral and mildly pleasant odors showed an increase in pleasantness ratings with subsequent encounters: mere exposure was working with these smells. But unpleasant and very pleasant odors remained unaffected by the frequency at which they had been encountered. It seems that for very nice smells and nasty ones, mere exposure does not work. One explanation for this is that we already like nice smells, so repeated exposure cannot make us like them more, and that nasty smells are nasty because we are supposed to find them aversive. This unpleasantness has survival value, and it would be a bad thing if we grew to like, for example, the smell of human excrement.

John Prescott and colleagues have also carried out an interesting study on mere exposure for smell, and the results are highly relevant to wine tasting. Their hypothesis was that attention might be an important element in mere exposure for odor. In an identification task, different smells were chosen either to be targets (the team would draw the subjects' attention to them) or nontargets (the subjects' attention was not drawn to them); otherwise, all the smells were exposed to the subjects uniformly. Liking increased only after exposure to the target odors. The team concluded that active attention could well be an important determinant of exposure effects. How does this apply to wine? If the mere exposure effect means that we like certain smells more only when we are paying attention to them, this suggests that someone looking for certain aromas in a wine—say, an expert trying to examine them analytically—will begin to like those aromas more. If Prescott and colleagues are right, only those elements of a wine's aroma that tasters are actively looking for will they begin to like more.

TOYING WITH FAULTS

One of the themes that have emerged in this book is the idea that sometimes fault compounds can be desirable—at the right level and in the right context. The best-known example of this is with volatile sulfur compounds ("reduction") in certain wines, particularly in Chardonnay. Many winemakers look to get a bit of "matchstick" reduction in their Chardonnays, following the lead of some of the top Burgundy estates such as Coche-Dury and Roulot, where matchstick in the right context is a complexing factor and a bit of a house style. It's only recently that toying with reduction like this has been widespread, and some complain that it is overdone. Winemakers in Australia have been criticized for their move to early-picked fruit coupled with deliberate reduction, resulting in a style that's been described as "lemon juice with matchstick." Reduction is also a style choice for some red winemakers who believe that starting a wine reduced can give it a long life, and that it will develop in interesting ways from that starting point. Another fault that some toy with is *Brettanomyces*. Some winemakers will use barrels that have gone a bit bretty as blending components, after first sterile filtering and/or treating them with Velcorin to get rid of any live cells that might bloom unpredictably in bottling. Their argument is that in the right context, brett can add a bit of seasoning. Yet another example is volatile acidity—it's normally a fault that people try to keep at as low a level as possible, but some are keen to avoid too little. That's because at a certain level it helps give extra lift and interest to the aroma of a wine. Above a certain level it's horrible, and there's also a legal limit, so care must be taken with this approach.

Chad Stock is a winemaker in Oregon whose wines are made under the Minimus label (he also makes the wines for Omero Cellars). Stock is keen to challenge the way that the wine trade deals with faults, which he thinks is too rigid. In May 2017, he presented a seminar in London titled "Truth, Beauty and Wine Faults," at which he encouraged participants to rethink some of their ideas on faults. He has made a number of one-off bottlings, including a wine called "I Have Brett, I Am Okay with That, I Am Enlightened," and others that flirt with reduction, oxidation, and volatile acidity.

"The wine trade in general is just getting much better at identifying these faults," says Stock. "That doesn't mean we understand them. There are certain styles and certain regions where some things are appropriate. Right now we are in this really bad place where it is all bad." Stock thinks that we are currently calling out what we have learned to identify as "faults" without thinking about the context.

> I see it more with winemakers and people who are in production than I do with wine writers, sommeliers, and importers. When you are from a wine production standpoint, you are more aware and have a heightened awareness of these things.... Oftentimes wine buyers are the most critical: they are not traveling to places like

wine writers and importers, who are less critical because they are traveling and tasting those wines with the entire context of the culture. They are bringing them back and selling them, and the buyers see these qualities in the wines and they are often very unaccepting.

Stock thinks volatile acidity (VA) is one of the best examples. "The general association with VA is ethyl acetate. No one talks about acetic acid." He suggests that depending on the source of the VA, you can have varying proportions of ethyl acetate and acetic acid.

> If it comes from lactic acid bacteria or acetic acid bacteria and it is not happening during the primary ferment, the wines just end up having high acetic acid. High acetic acid is quite sour and sweet at the same time, and once your acetic acid content goes up your pH goes down and the perceived acidity of the wine rises, and the wine becomes fresher. It's like adding a tiny bit of vinegar to food. If the ethyl acetate isn't there, it's a completely different conversation. I feel like the university and WSET [Wine and Spirit Education Trust, a British organization] systems are failing to educate at a little more detailed level and separate some of these things out.

Stock says the idea behind his seminar was to get people thinking. "It is important to have the skill and capability to identify these things. We want that. But if you find these faults, you have to step back and look at the wine from a pleasure standpoint. Does it taste good? Is it regionally appropriate? Is it appropriate for the culture where this wine is from? Is it balanced?"

AVOIDING FAULTS

Generally, though, people want to avoid faults and to minimize the presence of fault compounds in wine. To do this, a number of steps must be taken. The first is winery hygiene. Everything needs to be cleaned thoroughly, and if anything is brought in from outside, it must be screened first to make sure it isn't introducing taint compounds. Any wine additions, such as fining agents, need to be checked for purity. If there is any wood in the winery—whether part of the structure or in pallets, barrel stillage and chocks, or barrels themselves—this needs to be checked for the presence of taint compounds such as tribromoanisole. And the wine environment itself can discourage or encourage the growth of unwanted microbes such as *Brettanomyces*. Second, oxygen needs to be managed properly. During the early stages of a wine's life, oxygen is welcomed in many situations. It can remove phenolics from white wine must, and it helps yeast grow during fermentation. Very much less is needed after fermentation, and the delivery of oxygen to the developing wine needs to be closely monitored. Then, at bottling, it's possible to lose considerable quality and also to introduce bottle variation if oxygen pickup isn't controlled.

One of the major factors influencing the risk of the development of microbial faults is pH. If there's anything that encourages the wrong sort of bugs to grow, it's high pH. This is particularly true for bacteria. One of the benefits of low pH is that it causes more of the free SO_2 in the wine to be in the active molecular state, thus making it more effective.

Sulfur dioxide is one of the major defenses against the development of faults—both microbial faults and oxidation—and its correct use is one of the keys in minimizing existing faults. It's more effective to add SO_2 in one large dose rather than lots of small doses, where it all gets bound up (combining with certain wine components so that it is no longer in the active free form, but instead is bound and thus not useful). Indeed, one of the key quality-control measures that wineries should adopt is monitoring the ratio of free to total SO_2. "This is being used now by some wineries as their basic quality-control measure," says Adrian Coulter of the AWRI. "They know with several years of data what changes they'd expect to see in each wine over time. And if it goes out of this range they look to see what is going on." He adds that "an increase in bound sulfur dioxide is usually caused by acetaldehyde, and this is usually produced by yeasts. If it is not *Saccharomyces cerevisiae* (most of the time it isn't), then it can be a sign of brett. It's an early warning sign." The AWRI's Peter Godden adds, "If you need to add SO_2 because it is being bound, to keep the free SO_2 up, then the question is, what is binding it up? The free-to-total ratio tells you a lot about the wine's history."

Of course, for stylistic or ethical reasons, some producers prefer to work without SO_2 additions during fermentation, and a few will do without them even at bottling. And some may choose to work at higher pH, especially for red wines. In these cases, attention is needed to monitor what's taking place in the fermentation. The late Jules Chauvet, a winegrower and wine scientist from Beaujolais who is the unofficial father of the natural-wine movement, advocated paying great attention over the course of fermentation. He would monitor microbial populations under a microscope and use this information to choose when to intervene.

NO ROOM FOR COMPLACENCY

Despite the growing awareness of faults, we should not become complacent. Faults still scare winemakers, and rightly so. I asked Sam Harrop which faults worried him the most. "It's a difficult question," he replied.

They all scare me in equal measures if you want site expression and diversity in your wine. If you forced me to select one, assuming one has sound fruit, acetic acid bacteria would probably take it, with *Brettanomyces* a close second. If you get on to brett early enough it is not the end of the world, but it still masks terroir and prematurely ages the wine.

He is also concerned about volatile sulfur compounds (reduction) in some contexts. "Sulfides can also be a worry, but it depends on the wine style. In fruit-driven styles it can be a disaster, and yet it is so easily managed if the yeasts are healthy and happy. In certain less fruit-driven styles, in balance it can make the wine more interesting." He doesn't think wine faults are getting rarer.

> If anything they are becoming more of an issue. In lower-priced wines I am seeing more faults due to cutting back on winemaking inputs to save money. Oxidation, sulfides, and other faults from propagation [where winemakers grow up commercial yeasts in order to save money] are on the rise here. Sulfides with screw caps in aromatic styles continue to grow, especially in Europe. At the other end of the spectrum, as winemakers go for less intervention, there is a huge increase in faults. The middle ground is where faults may be falling, but the middle ground has been in good shape for a long time. It's important for you to understand that I talk about fault being a quality that dominates and masks the site and varietal expression. As we have discussed many times, while natural wines are a problem in this regard, I understand how consumers can enjoy them as the flavors are different, but [that has] nothing to do with terroir. Another big concern in this category for me is homogenization, and stylistically it is less diverse because of faulty compounds.

With the increasing adoption of screw caps in Australia and New Zealand, there may soon be a whole generation of winemakers who have grown up without exposure to cork taint. And with the success of the AWRI's brett program in Australia, there may soon be winemakers unfamiliar with the flavor this spoilage yeast imparts. This could have interesting implications for wine quality: what if faults creep back because winemakers are no longer vigilant in identifying them as they develop? This would be an unfortunate situation, although it's somewhat offset by regular exposure to European wines.

We began our in-depth look at the issue of wine faults, and more specifically of wine quality, by looking at the notion of beauty in wine. Is beauty simply the absence of flaws, or is it more nuanced? Can elements of what are generally considered faults be part of beauty? Could it be that our notion of perfection is itself flawed? Through the various chapters, which have looked at wine faults one by one, it has emerged that a simple, binary "faulty or not faulty" understanding of wine is extremely limited and needs some revision. We need to think more intelligently and holistically about the whole notion of wine quality. For wine is a wonderfully complex subject. Just as we think we are beginning to get somewhere, suddenly we are surprised and find that our understanding is inadequate. It is good to remain humble in the face of wine.

Notes

CHAPTER ONE

1. Salimpoor, V., M. Benovoy, K. Larcher, A. Dagher, and R. Zatorre. 2011. "Anatomically distinct dopamine release during anticipation and experience of peak emotion to music." *Nature Neuroscience* 14:257–262.

CHAPTER THREE

1. Serpaggi, V., F. Remize, G. Recorbet, E. Gaudot-Dumas, A. Sequeira-Le Grand, and H. Alexandre. 2012. "Characterization of the 'viable but nonculturable' (VBNC) state in the wine spoilage yeast *Brettanomyces.*" *Food Microbiology* 30:438–447.

2. Capozzi, V., M. Di Toro, F. Grieco, V. Michelotti, M. Salma, A. Lamontanara, P. Russo, L. Orrù, H. Alexandre, and G. Spano. 2016. "Viable but not culturable (VBNC) state of *Brettanomyces bruxellensis* in wine: New insights on molecular basis of VBNC behaviour using a transcriptomic approach." *Food Microbiology* 59:196–204.

3. Chatonnet, P., D. Dubourdieu, and J. Boidron. 1995. "The influence of *Brettanomyces/Dekkera* sp. yeasts and lactic acid bacteria on the ethylphenol content of red wines." *American Journal of Enology and Viticulture* 46:463–468.

4. Millet, V., and A. Lonvaud-Funel. 2000. "The viable but non-culturable state of wine micro-organisms during storage." *Letters in Applied Microbiology* 30:136–141.

5. Serpaggi et al., "Characterization of the 'viable but nonculturable' (VBNC) state."

6. Renouf, V., M. Perello, G. de Revel, and A. Lonvaud-Funel. 2007. "Survival of wine microorganisms in the bottle during storage." *American Journal of Enology and Viticulture* 58:379–386.

7. Zuehlke, J., and C. Edwards. 2013. "Impact of sulfur dioxide and temperature on culturability and viability of *Brettanomyces bruxellensis* in wine." *Journal of Food Protection* 76:2024–2030.

8. Gomez, D. 2012. "Identification and control of *Brettanomyces* in the vineyard and the winery." *On the Grapevine* (January–February):6–9.

9. Curtin, C., E. Kennedy, and P. Henschke. 2012. "Genotype-dependent sulphite tolerance of Australian *Dekkera (Brettanomyces) bruxellensis* wine isolates." *Letters in Applied Microbiology* 55:56–61.

10. Pradelles, R., A. Ortiz-Julien, H. Alexandre, and D. Chassagne. 2008. "Effects of yeast wallcomposition on 4-ethylphenol sorption in model wine." *Journal of Agricultural and Food Chemistry* 56:11854–11861.

11. Ferreira, D., D. Moreira, E. Costa, S. Silva, M. Pintado, and J. Couto. 2013. "The antimicrobial action of chitosan against the wine spoilage yeast *Brettanomyces/Dekkera*." *Journal of Chitin and Chitosan Science* 1:1–6.

12. Taillandier, P., C. Joannis-Cassan, J. Jentzer, S. Gautier, N. Sieczkowski, D. Granes, and C. Brandam. 2014. "Effect of a fungal chitosan preparation on *Brettanomyces bruxellensis,* a wine contaminant." *Journal of Applied Microbiology* 118:123–131.

CHAPTER FOUR

1. Schneider, V. 1998. "Must hyperoxidation: A review." *American Journal of Enology and Viticulture* 49:65–73.

2. He, F., N. Liang, L. Mu, Q. Pan, J. Wang, M. Reeves, and C. Duan. 2012. "Anthocyanins and their variation in red wines I. Monomeric anthocyanins and their color expression." *Molecules* 17:1571–160.

3. Boulton, R. 2001. "The copigmentation of anthocyanins and its role in the color of red wine: A critical review." *American Journal of Enology and Viticulture* 52:67–87.

4. Mattivi, F., R. Guzzon, U. Vrhovsek, M. Stefanini, and R. Velasco. 2006. "Metabolite profiling of grape: Flavonols and anthocyanins." *Journal of Agricultural and Food Chemistry* 54:7692–7702.

5. Waterhouse, A., and V. Laurie. 2006. "Oxidation of wine phenolics: A critical evaluation and hypotheses." *American Journal of Enology and Viticulture* 57:306–313.

CHAPTER SIX

1. Linderholm, A., C. Findleton, G. Kumar, Y. Hong, and L. Bisson. 2008. "Identification of genes affecting hydrogen sulfide formation in *Saccharomyces cerevisiae.*" *Applied and Environmental Microbiology* 74:1418–1428.

2. Linderholm, A., K. Dietzel, M. Hirst, and L. Bisson. 2010. "Identification of MET10–932 and characterization as an allele reducing hydrogen sulfide formation in wine strains of *Saccharomyces cerevisiae.*" *Applied and Environmental Microbiology* 76:7699–7707.

3. Cordente, A., A. Heinrich, I. Pretorius, and J. Swiegers. 2009. "Isolation of sulfite reductase variants of a commercial wine yeast with significantly reduced hydrogen sulfide production." *FEMS Yeast Research* 9:446–459.

4. Wilkes, E. 2016. "Closures: Is it the closure or the wine?" *Wine & Viticulture Journal* 31:22–25.

CHAPTER SEVEN

1. Chatonnet, P., S. Bonnet, S. Boutou, and M. Labadie. 2004. "Identification and responsibility of 2,4,6-tribromoanisole in musty, corked odors in wine." *Journal of Agricultural and Food Chemistry* 10:1255–1262.

2. Chatonnet, P., A. Fleury, and S. Boutou. 2010. "Identification of a new source of contamination of *Quercus* sp. oak wood by 2,4,6-trichloroanisole and its impact on the contamination of barrel-aged wines." *Journal of Agricultural and Food Chemistry* 58:10528–10538.

CHAPTER EIGHT

1. Westerling, A., H. Hidalgo, D. Cayan, and T. Swetnam. 2006. "Warming and earlier spring increase western U.S. forest wildfire activity." *Science* 313:940–943.

2. Australian Wine Research Institute. 2003. Annual Report. pp. 37–39.

3. Kennison, K., K. Wilkinson, A. Pollnitz, H. Williams, and M. Gibberd. 2009. "Effect of timing and duration of grapevine exposure to smoke on the composition and sensory properties of wine." *Australian Journal of Grape and Wine Research* 15:228–237.

4. Kennison, K., K. Wilkinson, A. Pollnitz, H. Williams, and M. Gibberd. 2011. "Effect of smoke application to field-grown Merlot grapevines at key phenological growth stages on wine sensory and chemical properties." *Australian Journal of Grape and Wine Research* 17:S5–S12.

5. Australian Wine Research Institute. 2003. Annual Report. pp. 37–39.

6. Ristic, R., P. Osidaxz, K. Pinchbeck, Y. Hayasaka, A. Fudge, and K. Wilkinson. 2011. "The effect of winemaking techniques on the intensity of smoke taint in wine." *Australian Journal of Grape and Wine Research* 17:S29–S40.

7. Fudge, A., R. Ristic, D. Wollan, and K. Wilkinson. 2011. "Amelioration of smoke taint in wine by reverse osmosis and solid phase adsorption." *Australian Journal of Grape and Wine Research* 17:S41–S48.

8. Singh, D., H. Chong, K. Pitt, M. Cleary, N. Dokoozlian, and M. Downey. 2011. "Guaiacol and 4-methylguaiacol accumulate in wines made from smoke-affected fruit because of hydrolysis of their conjugates." *Australian Journal of Grape and Wine Research* 17:S13–S21.

9. Wilkinson, K., R. Ristic, K. Pinchbeck, A. Fudge, D. Singh, K. Pitt, M. Downey, G. Baldock, Y. Hayasaka, M. Parker, and M. Herderich. 2011. "Comparison of methods for the analysis of smoke related phenols and their conjugates in grapes and wine." *Australian Journal of Grape and Wine Research* 17: S22–S28.

10. Dungey, K., Y. Hayasaka, and K. Wilkinson. 2011. "Quantitative analysis of glycoconjugate precursors of guaiacol in smoke-affected

grapes using liquid chromatography-tandem mass spectrometry based stable isotope dilution analysis." *Food Chemistry* 126:801–806.

CHAPTER NINE

1. Darriet, P., M. Pons, S. Lamy, and D. Dubourdieu. 2000. "Identification and quantification of geosmin, an earthy odorant contaminating wines." *Journal of Agricultural and Food Chemistry* 48:4835–4838.

2. La Guerche, S., S. Chamont, D. Blancard, D. Dubourdieu, and P. Darriet. 2005. "Origin of (-)-geosmin on grapes: On the complementary action of two fungi, *Botrytis cinerea* and *Penicillium expansum*." *Antonie Van Leeuwenhoek* 88:131–139.

3. Lisanti, M., A. Gambuti, A. Genovese, P. Piombino, and L. Moio. 2014. "Earthy off-flavour in wine: Evaluation of remedial treatments for geosmin contamination." *Food Chemistry* 154:171–178.

4. Weingart, G., H. Schwartz, R. Eder, and G. Sontag. 2010. "Determination of geosmin and 2,4,6-trichloroanisole in white and red Austrian wines by headspace SPME-GC/MS and comparison with sensory analysis." *European Food Research and Technology* 231:771–779.

CHAPTER TEN

1. Capone, D., K. Van Leeuwen, D. Taylor, D. Jeffery, K. Pardon, G. Elsey, and M. Sefton. 2011. "Evolution and occurrence of 1,8-cineole (eucalyptol) in Australian wine." *Journal of Agricultural and Food Chemistry* 59:953–959.

2. Osidacz, P., J. Geue, B. Bramley, T. Siebert, D. Capone, and L. Francis. 2010. "Exploring the influence of pepper, eucalyptus and smoky flavour compounds on consumer preferences of red wines." *AWRI Technical Review* 189:8–11.

3. Antalick, G., S. Tempère, K. Šuklje, J. Blackman, A. Deloire, G. de Revel, and L. Schmidtke. 2015. "Investigation and sensory characterization of 1,4-cineole: A potential aromatic marker of Australian Cabernet Sauvignon wine." *Journal of Agricultural and Food Chemistry* 63:9103–9111.

CHAPTER ELEVEN

1. Clark, A., D. Dias, T. Smith, K. Ghiggino, and G. Scollary. 2011. "Iron (III) tartrate as a potential precursor of light-induced oxidative degradation of white wine: Studies in a model wine system." *Journal of Agricultural and Food Chemistry* 59:3575–3581.

CHAPTER TWELVE

1. Marais, J. 1986. "Effect of storage time and temperature on the volatile composition and quality of South African *Vitis vinifera* L.cv. Colombar wines." In *The Shelf Life of Foods and Beverages,* ed. G. Charalambous. Elsevier, Amsterdam. pp. 169–185.

2. Ough, C. 1985. "Some effects of temperature and SO_2 on wine during simulated transport and storage." *American Journal of Enology and Viticulture* 36:18–22.

3. Puech, C., S. Vidal, J. Pegaz, C. Riou, and P. Uchot. 2006. "Effect of storage conditions on the evolution of bottled wines." *Journal of Viticulture and Enology of the Rhone Region,* 2006 ed.

4. Robinson, A., M. Mueller, H. Heymann, S. Ebeler, P. Boss, P. Solomon, and R. Trengove. 2010. "Effect of simulated shipping conditions on sensory attributes and volatile composition of commercial white and red wines." *American Journal of Enology and Viticulture* 61:337–347.

5. Meyer, D. 2002. "A study on the impact of shipping/transportation conditions and practices on wine." Document no 1.3.1/702.0001, Technology Exploitation Centre, South Africa.

6. Marquez, L., S. Dunstall, J. Bartholdi, and A. MacCawley. 2012. "Cool or hot: A study of container temperatures in Australian wine shipments." *Australasian Journal of Regional Studies* 18:420–443.

7. Du Toit, W., and C. Piquet. 2014. "Research Note: Effect of simulated shipping temperatures on the sensory composition of South African Chenin Blanc and Sauvignon Blanc wines." *South African Journal of Enology and Viticulture* 35:278–282.

8. WRAP. 2008. "Bulk shipping of wine and its implications for product quality." Report for GlassRite. WRAP, Oxon, UK.

CHAPTER THIRTEEN

1. Pickering, G., J. Lin, R. Riesen, A. Reynolds, I. Brindle, and G. Soleas. 2004. "Influence of *Harmonia axyridis* on the sensory properties of white and red wine." *American Journal of Enology and Viticulture* 55:153–159.

2. Pickering, G., D. Inglis, A. Botezatu, A. Beh, E. Humes, and I. Brindle. 2014. "New approaches to removing alkyl-methoxypyrazines from grape juice and wine." *Scientific Bulletin, Series F: Biotechnologies* XVIII:130–134.

3. Pickering, G., J. Lin, A. Reynolds, G. Soleas, and R. Riesen. 2006. "The evaluation of remedial treatments for wine affected by *Harmonia axyridis*." *International Journal of Food Science and Technology* 41:77–86.

4. Kögel, S., J. Gross, C. Hoffmann, and D. Ulrich. 2012. "Diversity and frequencies of methoxypyrazines in hemolymph of *Harmonia axyridis* and *Coccinella septempunctata* and their influence on the taste of wine." *European Food Research and Technology* 234:399–404.

5. Kögel, S., J. Gross, and C. Hoffmann. 2012. "Sensory detection thresholds of 'ladybird taint' in 'Riesling' and 'Pinot Noir' under different fermentation and processing conditions." *Vitis* 51:27–32.

6. Mohekar, P., T. Lapis, N. Wiman, J. Lim, and E. Tomasino. 2017. "Brown marmorated stink bug taint in Pinot Noir: Detection and consumer rejection thresholds of *trans*-2-decenal." *American Journal of Enology and Viticulture* 68:120–126.

CHAPTER SEVENTEEN

1. Wilkes, E. 2016. "Closures: Is it the closure or the wine?" *Wine & Viticulture Journal* 31:22–25.

Index